YORK NOTES

Gulliver's Travels

Jonathan Swift

Note by Mary Sewell

 Longman   York Press

Mary Sewell is hereby identified as author of this work in accordance with Section 77 of the Copyright, Designs and Patents Act 1988

YORK PRESS
322 Old Brompton Road, London SW5 9JH

PEARSON EDUCATION LIMITED
Edinburgh Gate, Harlow,
Essex CM20 2JE, United Kingdom
Associated companies, branches and representatives throughout the world

First published 1999

ISBN 0–582–38232–7

Designed by Vicki Pacey
Illustrated by Neil Evans
Phototypeset by Gem Graphics, Trenance, Mawgan Porth, Cornwall
Colour reproduction and film output by Spectrum Colour
Produced by Addison Wesley Longman China Limited, Hong Kong

C̲ONTENTS

PREFACE

York Notes are designed to give you a broader perspective on works of literature studied at GCSE and equivalent levels. We have carried out extensive research into the needs of the modern literature student prior to publishing this new edition. Our research showed that no existing series fully met students' requirements. Rather than present a single authoritative approach, we have provided alternative viewpoints, empowering students to reach their own interpretations of the text. York Notes provide a close examination of the work and include biographical and historical background, summaries, glossaries, analyses of characters, themes, structure and language, cultural connections and literary terms.

If you look at the Contents page you will see the structure for the series. However, there's no need to read from the beginning to the end as you would with a novel, play, poem or short story. Use the Notes in the way that suits you. Our aim is to help you with your understanding of the work, not to dictate how you should learn.

York Notes are written by English teachers and examiners, with an expert knowledge of the subject. They show you how to succeed in coursework and examination assignments, guiding you through the text and offering practical advice. Questions and comments will extend, test and reinforce your knowledge. Attractive colour design and illustrations improve clarity and understanding, making these Notes easy to use and handy for quick reference.

York Notes are ideal for:
- Essay writing
- Exam preparation
- Class discussion

The author of this Note is Mary Sewell MA, B Ed, senior examiner for GCSE literature. She is a tutor with the Open University, and delivers in-service training for teachers. The text used in these notes is the Penguin Classics edition, 1985, edited by Peter Dixon and John Chalker with an introduction by Michael Foot.

Health Warning: This study guide will enhance your understanding, but should not replace the reading of the original text and/or study in class.

Part one

Introduction

How to study a novel

You have bought this book because you wanted to study a novel on your own. This may supplement classwork.

- You will need to read the novel several times. Start by reading it quickly for pleasure, then read it slowly and carefully. Further readings will generate new ideas and help you to memorise the details of the story.
- Make careful notes on themes, plot and characters of the novel. The plot will change some of the characters. Who changes?
- The novel may not present events chronologically. Does the novel you are reading begin at the beginning of the story or does it contain flashbacks and a muddled time sequence? Can you think why?
- How is the story told? Is it narrated by one of the characters or by an all-seeing ('omniscient') narrator?
- Does the same person tell the story all the way through? Or do we see the events through the minds and feelings of a number of different people?
- Which characters does the narrator like? Which characters do you like or dislike? Do your sympathies change during the course of the book? Why? When?
- Any piece of writing (including your notes and essays) is the result of thousands of choices. No book had to be written in just one way: the author could have chosen other words, other phrases, other characters, other events. How could the author of your novel have written the story differently? If events were recounted by a minor character how would this change the novel?

Studying on your own requires self-discipline and a carefully thought-out work plan in order to be effective. Good luck.

Jonathan Swift was born in Dublin on 30 November 1667. Jonathan's father died before he was born and as a consequence he was raised in Cumbria for the first three years of his life. The family had no money and it was Godwin Swift, one of Jonathan's uncles, who ensured Jonathan was educated. He first went to Kilkenny School and later Trinity College at Dublin. Godwin died in 1688 and Jonathan Swift then went to work for Sir William Temple in Surrey as his private secretary. Sir William was a retired diplomat, now a leading member of the Liberal Party. It was here that Jonathan became interested in politics and political power and became ambitious. Here he composed three of his most famous **satires** (see Literary Terms), 'A Tale of a Tub' (1704), 'The Battle of the Books' (1704), and 'Discourse concerning the Mechanical Operation of the Spirit' (1704). It was during this time that Jonathan Swift first became ill with Ménière's disease, an illness which caused giddiness and vomiting. He tried returning to Ireland hoping a change of climate would help his condition, but later returned to work for Sir William. In 1695 Jonathan met Esther, whom he referred to as Stella. At this time, Stella was only fifteen years of age, and quickly became friends with Jonathan, who was also her tutor; this was a friendship that was to endure a lifetime.

The life of Jonathan Swift

In 1694 Jonathan was ordained a priest, and became Dean of St Patrick's Cathedral in 1713. After Sir William's death in 1699 Stella moved over to Ireland and stayed near Jonathan. There is some evidence that they secretly married in 1716, but the relationship was one of friendship. They saw each other every day and Jonathan wrote to her using intimate messages. He always composed a verse for her birthday.

In 1701 Jonathan, whose upbringing had been Whig (despite a Royalist and High Church background), wrote a pamphlet praising the Whigs (or Liberal) leaders. It was called 'A Discourse of the Contests and Dissensions between the Nobles and the Commons in Athens and Rome'. It was this pamphlet that made his political reputation. Jonathan experienced a tension between his political and religious beliefs and eventually, when the Whig ministry of Godolphin fell in 1710, Jonathan Swift changed his political allegiance and became a Tory. Jonathan Swift wrote some deeply religious pamphlets at this time such as: 'Sentiments of a Church of England Man', and the ironic 'Argument against Abolishing Christianity', and became the author of a Tory journal 'The Examiner' and 'The Conduct of the Allies'.

Jonathan Swift's later writing

In 1726 Jonathan wrote *Gulliver's Travels* which was published the same year and became a huge success. One of Jonathan Swift's friends wrote to him and said, 'From the highest to the lowest it is universally read, from the cabinet-council to the nursery.'

His later writings included *Short View of the State of Ireland* (1728), *A Modest Proposal* (1729), *Verses on the Death of Dr Swift* (1731) and *The Legion Club* (1736). Jonathan Swift was found to be suffering from a brain tumour that caused madness in the last three years of his life. His illness worsened and he died on 19 October 1745 and was buried under his own epitaph, which was written in Latin. W.B. Yeats translated it:

> Swift has sailed to his rest;
> Savage indignation there
> Cannot lacerate his breast,
> Imitate him if you dare,
> World-besotted traveller; he
> Served human liberty.

Jonathan Swift included two maps in his earlier version of *Gulliver's Travels*, and it was thought by readers that the lands of Lilliput and Brobdingnag actually did exist. We know that Jonathan Swift had read *New Voyage round the World* in 1717, a tale of a mariner's voyages fighting dangerous natural phenomena. Jonathan Swift loved travel and had explored most of Ireland. *Gulliver's Travels* is set in the South Seas or Pacific Ocean. We are given vague instructions as to actually where. In Lilliput we are told the latitude but not the longitude and we are left to presume the islands lie in the Indian Ocean. In Brobdingnag it is a monsoon which takes the ship off course from the Molucca islands into the Pacific. The journey reaches an imaginary continent – we must remember that this area remained unexplored in 1725. Conveniently another storm drives the ship to Laputa in the North Pacific, and the land of the Houyhnhnms is said to be 10° South of the Cape of Good Hope, or 45° South East of Madagascar. The maps in these notes are the original maps of *Gulliver's Travels*. Before we look at the imaginary locations of Lilliput, Brobdingnag, Laputa, Balnibarbi, Glubbdubdrib, Luggnagg and the land of Houyhnhnms, we should consider the influences on Jonathan Swift's own background which we find reflected in these mysterious lands.

BACKGROUND INFLUENCES

Gulliver's Travels is heavily **satirical** and **ironical** (see Literary Terms). It is therefore absolutely necessary to have a little understanding of the life and times of Jonathan Swift in order to understand the full implications of the novel.

The Church   At this time humankind was thought to be 'good'; individuals were motivated by sympathy, friendship and benevolence. It was thought that people were naturally logical, rational and virtuous in the same way that we feel today that we are liberal, generous and humanitarian.

However, Jonathan Swift did not agree with these views. He saw humankind as savage, driven by greed and lust, envy and avarice. This view, that people succumbed to the Seven Deadly Sins if they were not communicant members of the Church, is indeed severe, even for Jonathan Swift's times when preachers such as John Wesley found in *Gulliver's Travels* proof for the theory of Original Sin, which was the innate depravity of man, depicted by Adam eating the forbidden fruit.

In Jonathan Swift's novel we have plenty of evidence of moral criticism, but ironically for a book written by a clergyman, little evidence of religious faith. Jonathan Swift believed in the Anglican Church, established after 1688, which held a position of religious freedom for all, demonstrating neither a preference for Catholics nor Dissenters (Puritans).

After 1629 Parliament was dissolved by King Charles I as he prepared for a civil war between 'Cavaliers' (Scots Catholics and English Royalists) and 'Roundheads' (Scots Presbyterians and English Republicans). Oliver Cromwell, a Puritan who ruled England for ten years as Lord Protector, led the Roundheads.

In 1660, Charles II was crowned. This period was called the Restoration (i.e. the restoration of the British monarchy). The parliament was made up of Cavaliers, Tory squires and old Roundheads. There was some religious persecution of Dissenters. The Tory party found itself opposed by a Whig party who believed in religious toleration, especially for Protestants.

War with France

There were attempts to restore James, as a Catholic, to the English throne. War with France was inevitable to prevent Jacobitism (i.e. support of James). The duke of

Marlborough led Protestant Europe through the War of the Spanish succession (1701–13). This alliance of Whigs and Tories shared the responsibility for the government's money. War is expensive, and the English people simply wanted peace. The Treaty of Utrecht was therefore drawn up. It was during this time that Jonathan Swift changed his political allegiance from Whig to Tory.

Situation in Ireland

Ireland was at this time a poor country consisting mainly of Catholics who were anti-English. Indeed, over the decades, Ireland supported England's enemies in Spain and France. About once a year the Irish organised a rebellion and soldiers from England were sent to quell the riots. Each year some of the English stayed behind and over the years absentee landlords came to govern Ireland. She was denied any trading, and ruled by corrupt second-rate ambassadors, none of whom were Irish. Jonathan Swift, who believed in order and authority, saw Ireland as a land of neglect and decay. He felt he was living among 'beggars, thieves, oppressors, fools and knaves'. He firmly believed that the princes should protect their subjects and that the subjects in their turn should return a debt of loyalty to their princes. Jonathan Swift felt that the Anglo-Irish had been denied their rights under the Revolution Settlement. Jonathan Swift was particularly critical of Walpole's government and he produced pamphlets criticising matters in Ireland in the 1720s – the same time he wrote *Gulliver's Travels*.

Women in Jonathan Swift's Life

Jonathan Swift was a clergyman and a bachelor, but three women had an influence on his life and his career. The first was Jane Waring whom Jonathan Swift called Varina. He proposed marriage to her in 1695; she refused him but later changed her mind. However Jonathan Swift's pride had been hurt by the refusal, and he decided not to marry.

At Moor Park, Jonathan Swift was to educate Esther Johnson. Their friendship grew and Stella, as Jonathan Swift called her, followed him to Ireland. Stella became Jonathan Swift's lifelong friend. When she became sick and died, Jonathan Swift was so upset he could not attend the funeral.

During his visits to London in 1707–9 Jonathan Swift met the third woman in his life. Esther Van Lomriyh was the centre of Anglo-Irish society. Jonathan Swift called her Vanessa. Vanessa fell passionately in love with Jonathan Swift and followed him to Ireland in 1714. Jonathan Swift could not return the passion. Vanessa died in 1723 after a stormy love affair. He had written a poem 'Cadenus and Vanessa' which indicated the inequality of this love affair.

PART TWO

SUMMARIES

GENERAL SUMMARY

Gulliver's Travels is a **satirical** (see Literary Terms) novel. It works on two levels; the first a simple but exciting fairy-tale, the second a comment on Jonathan Swift's life and background. In his first voyage to Lilliput, Gulliver is shipwrecked. His captors are one twelfth of his own size but they manage to secure him as their prisoner. The social/political background of these people is similar to that found in England. Book I portrays the reigns of Queen Anne and George I. Gulliver is impeached and tried for treason, rather like the Earl of Oxford and Viscount Bolingbroke.

Once again, Gulliver is shipwrecked and accidentally abandoned by his shipmates, in what vaguely appears to be North America. In Book II the natives are twelve times bigger than Gulliver. Gulliver is adopted as a pet and exhibited as a sideshow. Once again Jonathan Swift uses him to make a political comment. This time Gulliver represents an eighteenth-century Englishman attempting to show morality, courage, honesty and realism to a benevolent though cynical giant monarch.

In Book III, pirates capture Gulliver and leave him on some small islands which we are told rather vaguely are near to Japan. This journey is different as Gulliver actually flies, on a flying island called Laputa. People obsessed by science, maths and astronomy populate this island. These people bully the people of Balnibarbi who live beneath them and literally in their shadow. Jonathan Swift uses this to make a comment on the ill-governed Britain of George I. In this book Jonathan Swift cleverly shows us how humankind's claim to be rational is false, and gives us numerous examples to illustrate this. From this island Gulliver visits Balnibarbi; on this island the 'immortals' live on to give advice to those who need it. Just when the reader begins to think that immortality may be a good idea, we are taken to Luggnagg where the people, Struldbruggs, are doomed to everlasting senility, a terrifying sight of physical decay and mental infirmity.

The voyage in Book IV returns us to a Utopian state, a land populated by two contrasting species. The Houyhnhnms are intelligent, superior, sensitive and empathetic, but have horse rather than human form. The opposite are the Yahoos who are dirty, savage, wild and primitive, but are human in form. However, the Houyhnhnms regard Gulliver as a Yahoo, and Gulliver is deeply sensitive of this. This journey affects Gulliver most deeply. On his return he seeks out conversations with his own horses and sees humankind as savage and barbaric just as the Yahoos were. Gulliver has become a man who has seen perfection and now seeks it everywhere.

Book I: A voyage to Lilliput

CHAPTER 1

How do the details of Gulliver's early life affect your understanding of him

Lemuel Gulliver begins his narrative with details of his childhood and training as a surgeon. After being unable to make a living on land he sets sail on 4 May 1699 from Bristol in the *Antelope*. Unfortunately the ship 'to the north-west of Van Diemen's Land' (p. 54) is shipwrecked and all Lemuel's companions lost. He wades ashore and falls asleep, but when he awakes he finds his hair and body are tied to the ground and he is unable to move. To his surprise he sees 'a human creature not six inches high' (p. 56). He attempts to escape but a volley of tiny arrows dissuades him from moving further. The inhabitants erect a stage and a tiny orator addresses the crowd. Gulliver fails to understand

Note your first impression of the people of Lilliput.

How do the people of Lilliput react to Gulliver?

what is being said; but is fed on meat and wine, which have been drugged, and subsequently falls asleep. The Lilliputians take Gulliver to their city on a specially constructed vehicle drawn by 'Fifteen hundred of the Emperor's largest horses, each about four inches and a half high' (p. 61). He is settled in 'a disused temple', where he is able to walk a little and sleep.

COMMENT

- We are almost catapulted into details of Gulliver's life up until he joins the *Antelope*.
- The details about the diminutive people of Lilliput add to the credibility of the story.
- Jonathan Swift has taken us into this magical world of miniature Lilliput, where tiny beings, who are described by Gulliver as being 'excellent mathematicians' (p. 61), live in an hierarchical state similar to that with which Gulliver is familiar.
- This chapter is largely innocent narrative and inspires the reader's confidence.

GLOSSARY

Leyden a university of medicine in Holland
Van Dieman's Land present-day Tasmania
made a shift made an attempt
computation calculation

CHAPTER 1 continued

spent with labour exhausted
ligatures ties
buff jerkin sleeveless yellow jacket
Signet Royal royal stamp
making water urinating
victuals food

CHAPTER 2 The chapter opens with an account of the way in which Gulliver dealt with his bodily functions and of his meeting with the Emperor, whose features are described as 'strong and masculine' (p. 65). Although Gulliver tries several European languages this is unsuccessful and the pair are left to communicate with signs and gestures. Gulliver demonstrates an act of mercy by releasing six ruffians, after first pretending to eat one of them. This gesture is well received by the court. Six hundred beds are combined to make Gulliver a bed and he, the 'Man-Mountain', is put on view to the public (p. 69). Two officers search Gulliver and make a list of his possessions; his sword and pistols are taken from him.

How much do you think the Emperor trusts Gulliver?

COMMENT • Gulliver and the imperial court find means of communicating and really get to know each other.
• Gulliver's 'needs' are all covered in this chapter. The reader is reassured as to his welfare.
• The Emperor has to make a law banning people from coming to see Gulliver more than once because it affects their work.

CHAPTER 3 The opening paragraph describes how the boys and girls play 'hide and seek' in Gulliver's hair, and goes on to describe the **satirical** (see Literary Terms) court where 'political candidates' perform tricks of rope dancing and jump like acrobats. Gulliver helps miniature horses perform by tying his handkerchief to sticks, making a platform for military displays, until a horse's hoof goes through the handkerchief and

Consider what Jonathan Swift is trying to tell us about promotions in this description.

Gulliver considers it unsafe. The Emperor is so
impressed that he is persuaded to grant Gulliver more
freedom of movement. Two days later, Gulliver is
requested to 'stand like a colossus, with my legs as far
asunder as I conveniently could' (p. 77) whilst the army
marchs between them. Gulliver's freedom is debated by
the government and as there is only one objection he is
granted his liberty after swearing to the eight

Who objects to conditions. The seventh sentences Gulliver to hard
Gulliver's labour in his leisure hours. Gulliver is allowed enough
freedom? food to support 1728 Lilliputians.

C OMMENT
- This chapter is full of **satire** and **irony** (see Theme
  on Satire and Irony).
- The people of Lilliput gain the Emperor's approval
  by demonstrating an acrobatic skill and therefore
  becoming courtiers or by leaping or crawling under a
  stick and winning a silken thread.
- Note the bizarre ritual Gulliver has to undergo in
  order to swear his obedience to the 'articles'.
- Look at the eight conditions set for Gulliver; he
  must:
  – Not leave Lilliput without permission
  – Give two hours' warning of a visit

- Keep to the main roads as he walks
- Take care as he moves
- Carry messages when required
- Defend Lilliput from its enemies
- Help with the building by lifting heavy stones
- Measure the kingdom

This chapter reflects King George's court under the Walpole government.

GLOSSARY   **Flimnap** a satirical remark about Sir Robert Walpole
strait narrow
summerset somersault
trencher flat board used for cutting meat
close chair sedan chair

CHAPTER 4

Note the description of the city. What effect does this have?

The capital Mildendo is described in detail by Gulliver when he visits the Emperor's palace. Reldresal, Principal Secretary of Private Affairs, interviews Gulliver, and tells him the political problems facing Lilliput. The two main are *Tramecksan* (these are the High-Heels), which party is the largest and the more traditional; and the *Slamecksan* (these are the Low-Heels) who are currently favoured by the Emperor and are in power.

List the beliefs of the Big-Endians and the Little-Endians.

Blefuscu is the one rival empire to Lilliput in this story. Blefuscu has supported the cause of the 'Big-Endians' against the 'Little-Endians'. The Big-Endians supported Blefuscu in their war against Lilliput. Reldresal tells Gulliver that they are in danger from an invasion and Gulliver readily agrees to help.

COMMENT

- This refers to political parties of Jonathan Swift's time. 'High-Heels' really refers to the Tories, and the 'Low-Heels' really refers to the Whigs.
- At this time the King favoured the Whigs, but the Crown Prince kept in favour with both parties and was said to 'hobble' with one heel higher than the other.

- The 'Big-Endians' were like the Catholics in England at this time, not allowed to hold high office.
- This chapter gives us an account of England and its historical factions – i.e. the 'bloody war' is the war of the 'Spanish Succession' (see Context).

GLOSSARY   **The Emperor's palace** a description of Hampton Court in 1700

Obstinate war the War of the Spanish Succession (1701–13)

intestine internal, domestic

Alcoran the Koran

CHAPTER 5

What causes the change in Gulliver's relationship with the Emperor?

Gulliver swims across the eight-hundred–yard channel between Lilliput and Blefuscu, hooks up the Blefuscudian fleet to cables and tows them back over to Lilliput. As a reward, Gulliver is made a Duke (*Nardac*), but decides not to help the Emperor any further to completely destroy Blefuscu. He claims he would 'never be an instrument of bringing a free and brave people into slavery' (p. 89). Gulliver begins to lose favour in Lilliput and he remarks 'Of so little weight are the greatest services to princes' (p. 89), indicating a break down in his relationship with the Emperor.

Try to list in chronological order all the things which lead to Gulliver's loss of favour.

A treaty is arranged with Blefuscu, but Gulliver's friendly attitude towards the people of Blefuscu, and his display of strength, seem to make matters worse. Further offence is caused when Gulliver puts out a fire in the palace by urinating on the flames. The Emperor and Gulliver part coolly, as a result of the influence of Gulliver's enemies who thought him guilty of treason.

COMMENT

- Note the way Gulliver's services are responded to by both the Emperor and the Empress.
- Note the examples of 'court intrigue' here.
- The incident of the palace fire is thought to represent the Treaty of Utrecht, where Bolingbroke and Oxford used illegal means to extinguish a conflagration.

GLOSSARY   **intercourse** a communication, conversation
embargo a ban on ships leaving a harbour or port
prow front of a boat
puissant powerful
encomiums speeches of praise or congratulations
junto a small political group
servile behaving like a slave
congratulate with to share a joy that is mutual

CHAPTER 6   Gulliver gives us a detailed account of some of the customs of the Lilliputians. Their dead are buried with their heads downwards, people are punished for making false accusations, embezzlers are executed as are people who demonstrate ingratitude! Atheists are not allowed public service. People in Lilliput are rewarded with special honours for being law-abiding. Good character is more creditable than high ability.

What happens to these children later?

Gulliver also deals with education. Young Lilliputians are educated in single-sex schools with slight differences between the boys' and girls' education. Children on farms are not taught in school at all.

Look up what a 'sprug' is.

List the factors which lead to a worsening of the relationship between Gulliver and the Emperor.

Gulliver's domestic details are given to us. We learn 'Two hundred sempstresses were employed to make me shirts', and 'three hundred cooks' (p. 100). This huge expense was recalled by Flimnap, the Lord High Treasurer to the Emperor, who claimed Gulliver had cost 'a million and a half of sprugs' (p. 101). This combined with a rumour about the close relationship between Gulliver and Flimnap's wife led to rift between Gulliver and the Emperor.

COMMENT   • Note the differences between our system of justice and that in Lilliput.
• Note the differences in child-rearing in Lilliput and in our society.

• This chapter has to be carefully considered; some parts seem a description of Utopia, others a very tongue-in-cheek commentary.

GLOSSARY   **ignominious** disgraceful
seventy-three moons about five and a half years
judicature the system of justice
weal welfare
concupiscence desire

CHAPTER 7

List the reasons given in the impeachment.

Gulliver, having given the reader an insight into the laws and customs of Lilliput, is about to experience them. He is the victim of a plot to impeach him for treason. He is accused of urinating on the palace, refusing to crush Blefuscu, and having contacts with the enemy.

The council delivers its punishment and Gulliver is told he is to be blinded and then starved to death. This would make his carcass 'more than half diminished' (p. 108) and thereby be less of a health hazard as it decays.

Three days later the impeachment is to be read to Gulliver and then the sentence carried out. Gulliver decides not to stand 'trial' before a court that has already decided his fate! He wades across the channel and is warmly received in Blefuscu, where they hold a reception 'which was suitable to the generosity of so great a prince' (p. 111).

COMMENT

• Note the changes in Gulliver's attitude towards the society of Lilliput.

• Consider the **irony** (see Literary Terms) in 'to signify the great *lenity* and favour of his Majesty and Council' (pp. 108–9).

• Gulliver does not tell the people of Blefuscu of his troubles in Lilliput.

Chapter 7 continued

GLOSSARY

common salutations customary greetings

pursuant to a legal term meaning 'following on from'

encomiums speeches of praise or congratulations

obnoxious unpleasant

no regular information no official notice

CHAPTER 8

Three days after arriving in Blefuscu, Gulliver finds a 'real boat' (p. 111). He manages to drag it ashore with the help of twenty Blefuscudian war ships. Meanwhile the Lilliputians send a message to Blefuscu, and demand that Gulliver be returned, 'bound hand and foot, to be punished as a traitor' (p. 113). The Monarch of Blefuscu replies saying that Gulliver's return is impossible. He offers Gulliver his 'gracious protection' (p. 114), but Gulliver's faith in promises has dwindled. Gulliver wants to take home a dozen Blefuscudians, but instead takes sheep and cattle. He sets sail on 24 September 1701, and after two days is picked up by an English ship. Gulliver has to show the captain the miniature sheep and cattle to convince him of his story. Six months later he arrives home, on 13 April 1792, and makes a living by showing his miniature sheep. Two months later, after speculating whether to breed the tiny sheep for their wool, he sets sail again on another adventure.

Compare the Emperor of Blefuscu with the Emperor of Lilliput.

Has Gulliver's attitude changed towards people in authority? If so, how?

COMMENT

- Note the coincidences – the upturned boat, and the English vessel returning home.
- When Gulliver is returned to his family, we are conveniently not told of his family's reaction to his voyage. We are only told that 'I took leave of my wife, and boy and girl, with tears on both sides' (p. 117).
- The lack of detail in Gulliver's homecoming contrasts dramatically with the detailed descriptions Gulliver has given of his journey to Lilliput.

GLOSSARY   **concourse** crowd
                  Cabal a group of people in a conspiracy
                  ancient a flag
                  upon the parish in need of charity
                  towardly dutiful

TEST YOURSELF (BOOK I)

 A *To whom or 'what' does the following refer.*

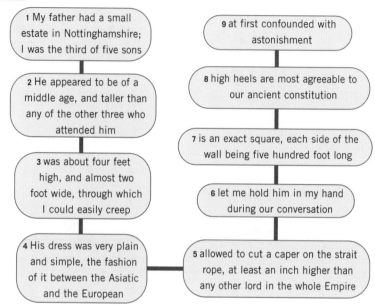

1 My father had a small estate in Nottinghamshire; I was the third of five sons

2 He appeared to be of a middle age, and taller than any of the other three who attended him

3 was about four feet high, and almost two foot wide, through which I could easily creep

4 His dress was very plain and simple, the fashion of it between the Asiatic and the European

5 allowed to cut a caper on the strait rope, at least an inch higher than any other lord in the whole Empire

6 let me hold him in my hand during our conversation

7 is an exact square, each side of the wall being five hundred foot long

8 high heels are most agreeable to our ancient constitution

9 at first confounded with astonishment

Check your answers on page 89.

 B *Consider these issues.*

a The description of the *Antelope* being wrecked in a storm. Do you find it believable?

b The lifestyle of the people of Lilliput compared with our own. What differences are there?

c What physical problems Gulliver encounters, and how the people of Lilliput solve them.

d How much trust there is between Gulliver and the Emperor. How is this developed?

e The way Gulliver's belongings are described. Why does Jonathan Swift do this?

f How Gulliver attempts to win the Lilliputians' affection.

g What we learn about life at court in Lilliput.

BOOK II: A VOYAGE TO BROBDINGNAG

CHAPTER 1

Note how Gulliver's curiosity leads him again into trouble.

Gulliver, travelling in the *Adventurer*, leaves Cornwall on 20 June 1702, and is blown off course and lands in the North Pacific on 16 June 1703. Gulliver goes ashore to find water but is abandoned by his shipmates who are chased by 'a huge creature walking after them in the sea' (p. 123). Gulliver turns to run away, but finds himself in a cornfield forty feet high which is about to be harvested by more of these huge men. Gulliver is taken home by one of them to show to his wife. The farmer is convinced Gulliver is a 'rational creature' (p. 127), but his wife is afraid at first and only when Gulliver displays good manners and amusing tricks does she relax and breastfeed her infant. This is described by Gulliver as 'nauseous' (p. 130). He has several terrifying experiences in the company of the cat, infant and small boy. He is awoken from sleep by two rats and is forced to slay one of them. Gulliver describes how he 'discharged the necessities of nature' (p. 133).

COMMENT

- In only one chapter, spanning two months, we are moved from the miniature world into a world of giants.
- The nautical detail adds to the 'realism' of the journal.
- The handkerchief used to make a platform for the military display is now used to wrap around Gulliver.
- Gulliver's physical needs are obviously to be a major theme in the books. Compare the detailed account in Book I, Chapter 1 with this one.

GLOSSARY

ague fever

overblow to blow over

spritsail/fore-sail the principle sail on the mast

mizen (mizzen) fore and aft sail

lanyard a short cord

whipstaff a small rod or mast

scudded moved swiftly in the wind
Great Tartary Land of the Tartar; any Asiatic empire
the frozen sea the Bering Sea
betwixt between
hinds farm servants

CHAPTER 2

Glumdalclitch, the nine-year-old daughter of the family, looks after Gulliver, whom she calls *Grildrig*. Gulliver says; 'To her I chiefly owe my preservation in that country: we never parted while I was there' (p. 134). Glumdalclitch's father decides to show Gulliver as an exhibit and he is taken in a little padded box to the town where he is put onto a table to perform to the audience. Eventually the two-month tour ends in *Lorbrulgrud*, the capital of this country, as Gulliver becomes ill. During the tour Gulliver is taught the language by Glumdalclitch, with whom he is forming an affectionate relationship.

The man who was the Lilliputians' major 'weapon' is now reduced to complete vulnerability in Brobdingnag.

COMMENT

- Note the way Gulliver is placed high upon the table to perform just as the Lilliputians performed for Gulliver.
- In Lilliput Gulliver's relationships are with people in power; politicians and ambassadors. In Brobdingnag his relationships are warmer and more intimate especially with Glumdalclitch.
- Gulliver's appearances in public in Lilliput displayed his strength and his capacity for power and protection. In Brobdingnag his public appearances are just the opposite and the reader feels Gulliver's vulnerability.

GLOSSARY

manikin/nanunculus from the Latin for 'dwarf'
ignominy shame
charged upon me as a reproach held against me as a disgrace
pumpion pumpkin
gimlet-holes small holes
palisadoed fenced
Sanson's Atlas seventeenth-century atlas

CHAPTER 3

Compare the initial reactions of the Lilliputians with the first reactions of the King.

Gulliver becomes further weakened, but his health is saved by his being bought by the Queen. Glumdalclitch is also to stay at Court to look after Gulliver. Gulliver confides in the Queen that his health is not good. The Queen, 'surprised at so much wit and good sense in so diminutive an animal' (p. 141) takes him under her protection. The King at first sees him as a *splacknuck* and then decides he is a clockwork toy. Three court scholars are called to question Gulliver and decide he is just a freak of nature. Gulliver is made a house and dines with the Queen and converses with the King. He is dropped into a bowl of cream by his enemy the dwarf – who is later 'soundly whipped' (p. 147). He then fights off huge flies and wasps, keeping some of the wasp stings to take back to England as a souvenir.

COMMENT
- Note how quickly Gulliver settles down to a comfortable life in the Palace.
- Gulliver is embarrassed by the King's observations on human society to begin with but later becomes angry with the lack of sensitivity.
- Consider the change in Gulliver's own attitude to his own size; 'the horror I had first conceived from their bulk and aspect was so far worn off' (p. 146).

• Note the change in Gulliver's attitude from being defensive of the English Court to agreeing that English Lords and Ladies are ridiculous.

GLOSSARY   **moidores** gold coins

vassal a servant who is protected by his master

scrutore a writing table

lusus naturae a freak of nature

craunch crunch

the *Royal Sovereign* a large British warship built in 1637

Gresham College The Royal Society of Science used this building from 1661–6

CHAPTER 4

Why do you think that the city is so graphically described? Is there a similar passage in the first journey?

Brobdingnag is described as a huge continent rather like North America; it is cut off on one side by stormy seas and on another by a thirty-mile-high range of mountains. Whales are eaten by the people of Lorbrulgrud. Gulliver travels in a specially made 'travelling closet' (p. 152). His view of the city is not a pleasant one, 'the most horrible spectacles that ever an European eye beheld' (p. 151). He describes cancer, lice, beggars and blisters. He is not impressed with either the King's palace or the chief temple, but is impressed by the King's kitchen, 'a noble building' (p. 153).

COMMENT   • Note the comparison in this chapter to England. The coach is compared to Westminster Hall, the chief temple to the steeple of Salisbury Cathedral, the King's oven to St Paul's cupola in London.
• Also note Gulliver's obsession with relating everything to size.

GLOSSARY   **tract** an area

no regular edifice Whitehall Palace was burned in 1698 shortly before Gulliver's first voyage

wen a blister or boil

sedan a type of carriage carried by men

the cupola of St Paul's the dome of St Paul's, completed by
Wren in 1710 is 112 feet wide and 365 feet high
battalia battle dress and formation

CHAPTER 5

*Compare
Gulliver's reaction
to the Maids of
Honour with his
observations in
Lilliput.*

Gulliver describes how his size gets him into 'several
ridiculous and troublesome accidents' (p. 154). He is
bombarded by dwarf apples and hailstones, picked up
by a spaniel, falls into a molehill, is pecked at by birds,
and is laid naked on the bosoms of the Maids of
Honour. The next episode deals with the execution of a
murderer, which Gulliver describes graphically but in a
detached way: 'The veins and arteries spurted up such a
prodigious quantity of blood' (p. 159). The Queen, in
an attempt to divert Gulliver, has a boat and a trough
made for him to sail in. Gulliver then describes his
abduction by a monkey, which attempts to feed him but
nearly chokes him, and finishes with an account of his
encounter with some cow-dung.

COMMENT

• Note the three episodes where Gulliver has intimate
  contact with the Maids of Honour. Jonathan Swift is
  making a comment on Court morals and is accusing
  them of immorality and sexual licence.

GLOSSARY

coined made up
jet d'eau a fountain
wherry a rowing boat

CHAPTER 6

Once again notice how the domestic detail of Gulliver's life reminds us of his tiny size.

The chapter opens with an amusing account of Gulliver making a comb out of the King's beard and chairs out of the Queen's hair. He also learns to play the spinet, but this serves to emphasise the **satire** (see Literary Terms) which is to follow. The King, in a series of interviews, asks a number of innocent yet searching questions. Gulliver attempts to support the argument for the worth of the undersized. He goes on to describe the English Parliament and the House of Peers and the House of Commons where he says they were 'always ready for the defence of their prince and country by their valour, conduct and fidelity' (p. 167). The King questions him on justice, the treasury and the army. Gulliver concludes with an historical account of his country over the last hundred years. However, the King, apparently unimpressed, declares that Gulliver's people must be 'the most pernicious race of little odious vermin that Nature ever suffered to crawl upon the surface of the earth' (p. 173).

COMMENT
- Gulliver uses his inventiveness to amuse the reader.
- Note how his speech convinces the King of his worth.
- Jonathan Swift builds up this chapter in a scene which was meant to inspire confidence and then shocks the reader with the King's final verdict.

GLOSSARY
levee a morning meeting held by a king
awl a tool for piercing wood
Demosthenes a humourless, yet skilled, Athenian orator (383–22BC)
Cicero Marcus Tullius Cicero (106–43BC) – an idealist and philosopher who was murdered by Antony, Octavian and Lepidus
plantations colonies
redound add advantage

CHAPTER 6 continued

slavish prostitute chaplains priests who gain power through
  flattering a lord
violently bent really very determined
pecuniary to do with money

CHAPTER 7

*Look at the way
Gulliver proudly
portrays England
in this sequence.*

Gulliver gives us reasons why he has been unable to
create a good impression of England; he blames the
constant questions of the King, 'that mighty monarch'
(p. 173). He makes allowances for the King's narrow-
mindedness by blaming the King's isolation – 'a King
who lives wholly secluded from the rest of the world'
(p. 174). Gulliver tries to please the King by telling him
the secret of gunpowder, but the King is horrified to
think that this is used to destroy nations. The King's
philosophy is that 'whoever could make two ears of
corn, or two blades of grass to grow upon a spot of
ground where only one grew before, would deserve
better of mankind' (p. l76). This is the simple adage
which is the central focus of this government's rule.

*In what ways are
the books different
from those
Gulliver was used
to?*

The people of Brobdingnag only learn morality, history
and poetry and the more practical forms of
mathematics. Philosophy and abstract ideas are not
valued. The laws are brief, and a well-disciplined
army is described in detail; the overall effect is of a
Utopian society. There are apparently no enemies;
earlier civil wars have been terminated by mutual
agreement.

COMMENT

• Note the attack Jonathan Swift makes on human
  weaknesses, being two-faced and behaving
  improperly.
• Note the contradiction in this chapter between
  Gulliver's declaration of 'an extreme love of truth'
  and his admission that his account has been made
  more favourable than 'the strictness of truth would
  allow' (p. 173).
• Jonathan Swift uses this chapter to further condemn
  hypocrisy and political corruption.

GLOSSARY   **rest with patience** to remain silent
              Dionysius Halicarnassensis a Greek historian of Rome (8BC)
              impotent powerless
              mechanical arts handicrafts
              transcendentals supernatural experiences
              mercurial a lively mind which often changes direction
              folios books
              happily tempered fortunately moderated
              composition agreement

CHAPTER 8   After two years in Brobdingnag, Gulliver longs to
              return home and to live his life on a normal scale.
              Glumdalclitch is unwell and they visit the sea.
              Here Gulliver is looked after by a trusted page who
              takes his box further along the beach but then falls
Gulliver appears   asleep. An eagle swoops down, picks the box up
to have travelled and then drops it and Gulliver into the sea. The
three hundred   box floats the right side up, but Gulliver spends an
miles in two   awful four hours in the water. Eventually he attracts
hours.   attention by flying a distress flag and is taken aboard
              an English vessel. The captain, Thomas Wilcocks
              of Shropshire, takes him home and gives him five
Compare the   shillings for his fare. Gulliver insists on telling the
account Gulliver captain his story and on showing him the evidence,
gives with that of some of which includes 'Four wasp stings, like
his arrival in   joiners' tacks; some combings of the Queen's hair,
Lilliput.   a gold ring ...' (p. 188).

COMMENT   • Note the difference in Gulliver's attitude when it is
                suggested that he is used for breeding, compared with
                his earlier wish to take away a dozen tiny Lilliputians.
              • Jonathan Swift portrays Gulliver's adjustment to size
                when he returns home, in a humorous way.

GLOSSARY   **tumbril** a two wheeled cart
              the cataract of Niagara the great waterfall in Canada
              raillery witty criticisms
              Phaethon (Greek mythology) son of the Sun god

Tonquin Tongking in Vietnam
New Holland Australia
the Downs off the South Coast of England
freight a means of paying his fare

To whom' does the following refer.

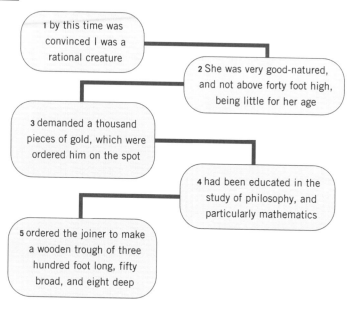

1 by this time was convinced I was a rational creature

2 She was very good-natured, and not above forty foot high, being little for her age

3 demanded a thousand pieces of gold, which were ordered him on the spot

4 had been educated in the study of philosophy, and particularly mathematics

5 ordered the joiner to make a wooden trough of three hundred foot long, fifty broad, and eight deep

Check your answers on page 89.

 Consider these issues.

a How Gulliver's character is portrayed as restless. What other characteristics does Gulliver portray in this book?

b Why Glumdalclitch becomes Gulliver's friend. Consider how her character is described and developed by Jonathan Swift.

c How Gulliver's life changes once he is in court.

d Gulliver is disgusted and horrified by several very common spectacles. Look again at how these incidents are described. Why do you think Jonathan Swift does this?

Book III: A Voyage to Laputa

CHAPTER 1   Captain William Robinson employs Gulliver to be ship's surgeon on the *Hope-well*. They sail on 5 August 1706 for the East Indies. During a delay at Tonquin Gulliver takes out a sloop which is boarded by pirates, and his men are taken prisoner. After some discussion between Dutch and Japanese officers, Gulliver is set adrift in a small canoe, which he later beaches in a remote island. As he walks along in the heat of the sun he suddenly finds himself in shadow. The sun has been eclipsed by 'a vast opaque body' (p. 198). He looks up to see it is a huge flying island; he attracts the inhabitants' attention by waving and bowing and is pulled aboard.

Notice the reference to 'supplicating posture' (p. 200). Where else has Gulliver behaved like this?

COMMENT

- Note the attitudes of the Dutch and Japanese officers; this reflects Jonathan Swift's own attitude towards the Dutch whom he hated.

GLOSSARY

Fort St George the great Indian port of Madras was developed in 1640 from a station of the East India Company
power to traffic authority to trade
new manned with an independent crew

CHAPTER 2   The people on the flying island of Laputa are the strangest we have yet met. They carry their heads on one side and their eyes look in different directions. All these inhabitants are attended by *flappers*, who smack their masters in order to attract their attention; a blow to the mouth encourages speech whereas a blow to the ears indicates they should listen. These people are besotted with astrology and music and their clothes bear musical and astrological symbols.

The King orders the court to entertain its inhabitants with 'music of the spheres' (p. 204), which is a noisy and unmelodious performance. From below the island hauls up petitions from the discontented mainland, but little is actually addressed as all ideas are expressed in either mathematical or musical terms. These people are not practical and are unable to think logically. We are given several examples of this, such as the defective buildings and that Gulliver's new clothes fail to fit. Gulliver claims the inhabitants have a complete lack of imagination.

Compare the role of women here and in Lilliput.

The women of this island are left to their own devices as the men are simply obsessed by the possible destruction of the island. The women are kept in luxury and idleness on the island and are visited by admirers from the mainland below.

COMMENT

- Note how we have moved from the physical differences of the miniature and gigantic into differences of intellect and understanding.
- In this world, Jonathan Swift cynically portrays the clever and top level of society to be disassociated from reality. The less intelligent are actually more practical, and more capable of running the island.

GLOSSARY

external taction physical touch
rhomboids quadrilaterals with opposite sides and angles equal
hautboys instruments now known as 'oboes'
quadrant an instrument for measuring altitude by angles
the music of the spheres the planets were once believed to

create music as they moved, but this sound was inaudible to
the human ear

bevel a slant

judicial astronomy fortune telling using the position of the stars

effluvia outpouring of vapour or solid matter

perihelion the point nearest to the sun in a planet's orbit

CHAPTER 3

*Gulliver appears
to be measuring
again. Why is this
important?*

Gulliver tells us in detail about the island's magnetic
system and propulsion. He also describes how the King
of Laputa controls the people on Balnibarbi – the land
which lies beneath the floating island. He does so by
obscuring the sun and rain, or even by landing the
island on them. The cities defend themselves by hiding
under natural rocks or by being protected by massive
towers specially built for the purpose.

COMMENT

• Note the cynical view expressed by Jonathan Swift in
this chapter the relationship between the governed
and the governors.

GLOSSARY

astrolabes instruments for measuring the altitude of the stars

demesne personal estate

backs as in 'fire-back' in hearths

CHAPTER 4

*Notice the contrast
between Munodi's
palace and the
land outside.*

Gulliver asks for permission to visit Balnibarbi where
he finds extreme poverty and distress. The people are
'generally in rags' (p. 219) and look desolate and
miserable. Gulliver stays with Lord Munodi where he
finds just the opposite; Lord Munodi's estate is well
kept and orderly but Munodi himself is hated by the
people. Up above on the island, new rules for running
Balnibarbi have been passed, to modernise their
lifestyles; meanwhile below 'the whole country lies
miserably waste, the houses in ruins, and the people
without food or clothes' (p. 222). Gulliver visits the
main Academy of Projectors and finds even more
bizarre practices; poor design and faulty structures are
replacing effective and working buildings. Munodi has

taken on one of these to replace a good working mill on his estate.

COMMENT
- This chapter parodies (see Literary Terms) eighteenth-century Ireland where the poor starved whilst the economists argued over political reforms. Jonathan Swift wrote *Modest Proposal* (1729) which was intended as a direct parody of this chapter.

GLOSSARY

Lord Munodi may be a reflection of Jonathan Swift himself, who kept his house in order

CHAPTER 5

Gulliver visits the Academy of Lagado, where the academics in some five hundred rooms explore the most extraordinary research. The list includes: the extraction of sunlight from cucumbers, making pillows from marble, abolishing words and replacing them with actions in the language, turning ice to gunpowder, and the mixing of paint by a blind man. Other schemes include an architect who devises house building by starting with the roof, a new form of ploughing by letting pigs roam free, the joining of a sundial to a weathercock to link sunshine with wind, and a doctor who cures colic by using a pair of bellows. In the department of speculative learning Gulliver watches a word machine operated. In the school of languages three professors reduce all words to monosyllables and eliminate all verbs. In the mathematical school propositions are literally swallowed by writing them on wafers which are eaten!

What were coloured silks produced from? Read p. 225 again to find out.

COMMENT
- Note Jonathan Swift's tongue-in-cheek condemnation of academics.
- Many of these bizarre examples were based on actual papers produced by the Royal Society, so once again Jonathan Swift uses satire (see Literary Terms).

GLOSSARY

nitre potassium nitrate

cephalic tincture essence distilled from brains

bolus a large pill

CHAPTER 6 This is simply a further account of the Academy. We are told that the professors seem to be 'wholly out of their senses' (p. 232). Here sensible ideas are treated as abnormal. There is an inversion of the satirical elements. A doctor has devised physical ways of bringing about improved government by shortening debates, prompt action by ministers and an insistence that members votes in an opposite direction to the views they have expressed. The most peculiar 'clue' is to surgically fuse two halves of brains that hold opposite opinions, therefore bringing about political reconciliation. Taxes are levied – after neighbours assess each others' vices, or after people assess their own virtues.

Gulliver assists one professor by contributing the idea that men could be taken away and their letters and papers searched for evidence of spying. This is a direct reference to 'the Kingdom of Tribnia (Britain), by the natives called Langden (England)' (p. 236).

COMMENT • Note the impossibly ideal schemes of government.
• Compare this with the disease-ridden administration.

GLOSSARY chimeras wild ideas
peccant morbid
cephalalgics, icterics medicines for headache and jaundice respectively

CHAPTER 7 Gulliver sets sail for Maldonada, via Luggnagg and from there to Glubbdubdrib, the Island of *Sorcerers* or *Magicians*, which lies fifteen miles to the south-west. The dead are called up to serve the governor for twenty-four hours; this makes Gulliver's 'flesh creep with a horror' (p. 239). Brutus is one of these ghosts and is described with admiration. Other characters Gulliver experiences are Alexander, who discloses to Gulliver that the real reason for his death is that he was

Who are the
exclusive group of
six? Look back to
page 241.

drunk, Caesar and Pompey, who confront each other, and the Senate of Rome which faces a modern parliament. Gulliver is told of the *sextumvirate*, an exclusive group of the ex-leaders 'to which all the ages of the world cannot add a seventh' (p. 241).

COMMENT

- Note how this story actually links with the real world of Jonathan Swift (see Context).
- The grisly spectacle of ghosts is the most hard scene we have witnessed so far.

GLOSSARY

Alexander the Great died in 324BC after defeating Darius of Persia in 331BC

Hannibal Carthaginian general who took 60,000 men and crossed the Alps on elephants to invade Italy

Caesar and Pompey two famous Roman leaders

Socrates a Greek philosopher who took poison in 399BC after being sentenced to death for impiety

Brutus committed suicide after murdering Caesar

Junius Lucius Junius Brutus, first Consul of Rome 509BC after expelling Tarquin rulers. Had his own sons killed for treason

Epaminondas a Greek general about 360BC. Commander of Thebes, known for his honesty

Cato the younger leader of the Roman aristocracy who committed suicide in 46BC after the fall of Pompey

Sir Thomas More Great English scholar and author of *Utopia*. He was put to death for refusing to acknowledge Henry VIII as head of the Church of England, and was later canonised

CHAPTER 8

Two villagers and
a courtier are
deliberately placed
together here. Why
do you think this
is?

Gulliver calls up Homer and Aristotle, who are attended by hosts of ignorant commentators who declare they are now ashamed of their criticisms of these great ancients. Homer finds that two of his critics lack poetic appreciation. Aristotle accuses his of being stupid. Gulliver is disappointed when he explores the ancestry of ancient noble families where he finds the lineage interrupted by 'pages, lackeys, valets'

CHAPTER 8 continued

(p. 244), and is disgusted to find that many great men have acquired their greatness and wealth by engaging in 'sodomy or incest' (p.245), prostitution and poisoning.

COMMENT
- Note how this passage comments on every kind of vice and injustice.
- This is Jonathan Swift's most damning comment on Europe past and present.

GLOSSARY
Didymus (63BC–AD10) a scholar
Eustathius Archbishop of Thessalonica. Author of *Homer*
Scotus a Franciscan scholar (1265–1308)
Ramus a French philosopher (1515–72)
Descartes and Gassendi two French philosophers of the seventeenth century
Epicurus Greek philosopher (343–270BC)
vortices circular movements of water
helot a Greek slave
Agesilaus King of Sparta (397–360BC)
Polydore Virgil an Italian who wrote *History of England* (1534)
panderism serving the evil desires of another
Actium famous sea battle
libertina the Latin name for a freed woman

CHAPTER 9
Gulliver sets sail on a one-month voyage to Luggnagg. He tells his story to an official on arrival and is then confined for two weeks until he receives royal permission to visit the King to '*lick the dust before his footstool*' (p. 249). This is a very literal function and leaves the visitor petitioner with a mouth full of dust, which ensures they cannot speak when they eventually see the King. The King disposes of his enemies by poisoning the dust. Gulliver is received well by the King and stays for three months.

COMMENT
- Note how Gulliver, who is now travelling to Japan, has assumed the identity of 'a Hollander' (p. 248).

GLOSSARY   **trade wind** a wind which always blows in the same direction

                   a cable's length about six hundred feet

CHAPTER 10

Gulliver has heard of a race of immortals known as Struldbruggs, and is delighted to be able to speak to them. This joy quickly turns to horror as he finds them not to be wise but 'not only opinionative, peevish, covetous, morose, vain, talkative, but incapable of friendship, and dead to all natural affection' (p. 257). This has affected the Luggnaggians considerably; they now have no desire to go on living, as all they can look forward to is an endless old age.

Compare the last sentence in this paragraph with Gulliver's previous ideas on immortality.

COMMENT

- Gulliver has good intentions of using his meeting with the Struldbruggs to stop the progressive corruption of the human race.
- This passage could be interpreted as a sermon by Jonathan Swift to help people come to terms with death and welcome the Christian prospect of a life after death.

GLOSSARY   **I discovered my admiration** at this time it would mean I expressed surprise

                 memorials remembered memories

                 common imbecility foolishness

                 meres eastern boundaries

                 always upon the flux constantly changing

                 engross to monopolise

CHAPTER 11

Gulliver refuses a job, the first he has been offered on his travels, by the King of Luggnagg and sets sail for Japan on 6 May 1709. When he arrives at Nangasac he takes a job as a ship's surgeon on a Dutch ship bound for Amsterdam. Gulliver works hard to pass

Are you satisfied   himself off as a Dutchman and claims to have relatives
with this   in Holland. He travels from Amsterdam back home
description of   after an absence of five years and six months. At
Gulliver's   Redriff he finds 'my wife and family in good health'
homecoming?   (p. 263).

COMMENT   • Gulliver is still pretending to be a Dutchman, for his
own safety.

GLOSSARY   **Yedo** Tokyo

Guelderland historically part of the Netherlands, now known as
Arnhem

Guinea New Guinea, north of Australia

TEST YOURSELF (BOOK III)

 A *'To whom' or 'what' does the following refer.*

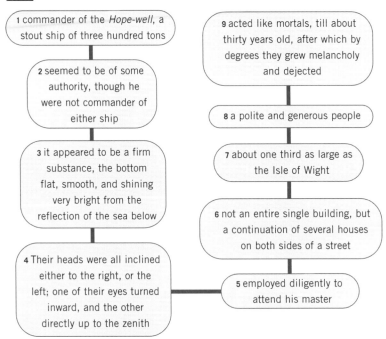

1 commander of the *Hope-well*, a stout ship of three hundred tons

2 seemed to be of some authority, though he were not commander of either ship

3 it appeared to be a firm substance, the bottom flat, smooth, and shining very bright from the reflection of the sea below

4 Their heads were all inclined either to the right, or the left; one of their eyes turned inward, and the other directly up to the zenith

5 employed diligently to attend his master

6 not an entire single building, but a continuation of several houses on both sides of a street

7 about one third as large as the Isle of Wight

8 a polite and generous people

9 acted like mortals, till about thirty years old, after which by degrees they grew melancholy and dejected

Check your answers on page 89.

 B *Consider these issues.*

a 'The natural love of life gave me some inward motions of joy, and I was ready to entertain a hope' (p. 199). How was this later demonstrated?

b The lifestyles of the people on the flying island and the inhabitants of Balnibarbi.

c Why Gulliver describes some of the 'projects' undertaken by the Academy in such detail.

d The contrasts between the inhabitants of Laputa with their contempt for geometry and the inhabitants of Balnibarbi who adore academic life.

e Why Gulliver's excitement at the prospect of living forever changes as he observes the Struldbruggs.

BOOK IV: THE COUNTRY OF THE HOUYHNHNMS

CHAPTER 1

On 7 September 1710 Gulliver sets sail from Portsmouth, as Captain of the *Adventure* to the South Seas via the West Indies. Sickness strikes the ship and some of the crew are lost. Those crew members are replaced in the West Indies by buccaneers in disguise. These men quickly corrupt the rest of the crew and mutiny. Gulliver is confined to his cabin for weeks and then marooned in an unknown country.

He comes across a group of 'ugly monsters' (p. 270) who are prepared to attack him like savages, but he is rescued when they run away at the sight of a horse. The horse inspects him and then discusses him with another horse! Gulliver decides they must be magicians in disguise and makes a polite speech to them. They teach Gulliver two words: *Yahoo* and *Houyhnhnm*, and then Gulliver is signalled by the grey horse to go with him.

Why do you think this speech is comic?

COMMENT
- We are given a full picture of Gulliver's state of mind prior to the mutiny.
- The 'ugly monsters' have human form and the creatures with human characteristics are horses.

GLOSSARY

Teneriffe largest of the Canary Islands
the bay of Campechy at the south end of the Gulf of Mexico
Barbadoes an island in the West Indies
Madagascar an island off the East Coast of Africa
lading a cargo
pastern part of the horse's foot between the fetlock and hoof
metamorphosed themselves changed shape

CHAPTER 2

Gulliver goes with the horses and is led to a stable. Gulliver still expects to meet the human owners of these horses and eventually realises that this is not to be the case. The grey horse introduces Gulliver to a mare and foal and then puts Gulliver next to a Yahoo so that he may be compared to them. Gulliver is relieved that he wears clothes which helps to distinguish him from 'this abominable animal, a perfect human figure; the face of it indeed was flat and broad, the nose depressed, the lips large, and the mouth wide' (p. 276).

Gulliver is unable to eat either the ass-meat offered to the Yahoo or the oats the Houyhnhnms eat. Gulliver accepts a bowl of milk and makes himself some porridge. A sledge drawn by four Yahoos brings an elderly horse to dine. Gulliver sleeps on a bed of straw between the house of the Houyhnhnms and the stable of the Yahoos.

How effective is this comparison?

COMMENT
- Note Gulliver's dramatically incorrect behaviour in offering his presents – paltry gifts one would offer to savages.
- The complete change of animal and human behaviour is so well managed by Jonathan Swift as to be credible.

GLOSSARY   **necromancy** communication with the dead
                      withes pliable twigs formed into halters
                      sorrel nag a small reddish brown horse
                      bosses seats made of straw from Holland

CHAPTER 3   Gulliver and 'master' communicate and Gulliver learns the language by imitating the nasal sounds expressed by

What is meant by 'appearance of reason'?

the horse. The grey horse is obsessed with observing the differences between Gulliver and the Yahoos; he is 'extremely curious to know from what part of the country I came' (p. 281). Gulliver is seen as a separate species due mainly to his clothes. However one morning the sorrel nag, Gulliver's valet, sees him undressed and goes to tell his master. Gulliver demonstrates how he is able to take off and put on his clothes. Fortunately the grey horse seems to be more interested with Gulliver's intellect than his physical deficiencies.

Gulliver gives the grey horse an account of how he came to be there, but the horse thinks that he is telling lies, as he puts it, things *'which are not'* (p. 281). The horse cannot comprehend another country being beyond the sea, or that the sea may be travelled in boats made by creatures like the Yahoos, and although he sees the physical likeness with the Yahoos, he is prepared to ignore it for the meantime.

At the end of the chapter the Houyhnhnms conclude that without clothes and Gulliver's preference for walking on his hind legs, he would be a Yahoo.

COMMENT

- The only differences identified by Jonathan Swift between man and the animals is that men wear clothes and write their thoughts on paper.

GLOSSARY

their language approaches … German a comparison by Gulliver of the horse speech to German. This is thought to be a reference to Emperor Charles V (1500–58), who is said to have said that he would speak to his mistress in Italian, his God in Spanish and his horse in German

CHAPTER 4

What Gulliver tells his 'master' is incomprehensible to him. Gulliver explains that horses in England are groomed and cared for by Yahoos. Unfortunately,

What reaction did the Houyhnhnms have?

Gulliver goes on to explain spurs and castration, and his own embarrassment at the grey's 'noble resentment at our savage treatment of the Houyhnhnms' (p. 288) is obvious. Gulliver tries for a third time to explain his background and his journey but finds difficulty in explaining why some of his crew had been punished and banished. It takes several days to explain this, but eventually the Houyhnhnm seems to be able to distinguish the human race, and wants to know more about Europe and England.

COMMENT

- Jonathan Swift develops the line of inquiry from Gulliver to more general issues and then to European society.
- Jonathan Swift uses Gulliver to display embarrassment at the treatment of horses at home, when it parallels exactly the Houyhnhnm treatment of the Yahoos.

CHAPTER 5

List what brought the master to this decision.

In the next two paragraphs Gulliver explains the causes of war and therefore human history at its worst. Gulliver talks about England in particular and lists the causes of war and how the soldier is really just a trained killer. The grey horse cannot understand how the European is so strong when man is obviously physically inferior. This leads Gulliver into a detailed account of warlike operations and strategies, but the grey is unimpressed and concludes that these people (Europeans) must be more corrupted than the naturally vicious Yahoos.

The Houyhnhnms ask about the law and Gulliver gives a very black and white account of the legal profession, explaining that English law is based on precedent, which makes certain that whatever has been done in the past may be done again and that the lawyers 'take special care to record all the decisions formerly made against common justice' (p. 296). In this chapter the Yahoos remain in the background.

CHAPTER 5 continued

COMMENT
- Note the detailed description Gulliver gives of the legal system in England, and how lawyers are trained to prove the opposite of truth in courts of law.
- Note too the English use of 'precedents', where what has gone before will always be used as a yard stick. In the cases where injustice has prevailed, the worst of errors are thereby perpetuated.
- Look at the use of legal terms to confuse the ordinary person.
- Consider Gulliver's assertion that lawyers are generally the most ignorant and prejudiced professionals.

GLOSSARY
Revolution revolution of 1688 in which James II was dethroned
injure the *Faculty* discredit the profession
abroad out in the fields

CHAPTER 6
In this chapter Gulliver tries to describe money, how it is minted, and how it is used. He describes the difference in wealth: 'the bulk of our people was forced to live miserably, by labouring every day for small wages to make a few live plentifully' (p. 298). He claims that man's needs are more luxurious and this leads to degeneration, 'diseases, folly and vice' (p. 299). The Houyhnhnms cannot understand disease, and when Gulliver explains ill health he includes an attack on his own profession, and gives examples of unprofessional practice.

How many of these incidents are you able to remember?

The Houyhnhnms ask him to explain the expression *Minister of State*. The chapter concludes with Gulliver's scathing account of ministerial functions, and even more derisory remarks on the nobility.

COMMENT
- This is Jonathan Swift's most scathing attack on English society and gives us an insight into the state of England under Queen Anne.

- Note the contrast that Gulliver portrays between the desperate corruption in England and that of the lifestyle of the depraved Yahoos.
- Note the exaggeration of all Gulliver's examples.

GLOSSARY

suborning giving false evidence

clyster an enema

CHAPTER 7   Gulliver explains why he has portrayed England and the English in such a dreadful way; he feels he has found faults within himself. Gulliver also feels a loyalty towards the Houyhnhnms which has resolved him not to return home but to stay in this land of honesty and virtue.

The grey reflects upon the English. He declares they must have limited intellect which they use to increase corruption. The grey concludes from Gulliver's similarity to the Yahoos that there is an intellectual similarity also. He now sees the Yahoos as quarrelsome, selfish and greedy; these are all similar vices to those *What comparisons* expressed by Gulliver. The master goes on to describe *are intended to be* the way in which the Yahoos collect shiny pebbles and *drawn here?* jealously guard them, causing tribal wars. The Yahoos eat anything they can steal, and after they have overeaten they need laxatives; nearly all the ill health they experience is due to overeating.

The grey goes on to describe sexual promiscuity and dirtiness among the Yahoos, and how hard work cures an attack of low spirits.

COMMENT
- Note the direct comparison between shiny pebbles and diamonds. This is Jonathan Swift's **satirical** (see Literary Terms) comment on avarice, jealousy and greed – all human vices for the reader to reflect on.
- Gulliver portrays the human race as a people who are intelligent but overindulgent and wicked.

- The master portrays the Yahoos as cunning and savage animals who, **ironically** (see Literary Terms), demonstrate the same vices as man.

GLOSSARY

entire congruity exact similarity of shape
no pretence to challenge no grounds to claim
spleen this is referred to as an ailment suffered by Yahoos: in Jonathan Swift's time it was common, a mixture of low spirits and hypochondria – a sort of depression

CHAPTER 8

This chapter is equally divided between the Yahoos and the Houyhnhnms.

Gulliver is determined to take a closer look at the Yahoos, hoping to make comparisons to prove the horses wrong. As he is bathing, a young Yahoo female accosts him and this gives the horses even more proof that he is indeed a Yahoo. Interestingly, Gulliver seems to have enjoyed the encounter: he describes her as not 'altogether so hideous' as the others and that she 'stood gazing and howling all the time I was putting on my clothes' (p. 315).

Gulliver turns his attention to the Houyhnhnms, who seem to have no differences of opinion, which means they have no need for book learning or philosophy, and, as we learn at the end of the chapter, their national parliament only needs to meet every four years to share oats, Yahoos, cows and so on equally amongst themselves.

The Houyhnhnms offer friendship and benevolence in all their relationships, their offspring are brought up without close emotional attachments. Marriages are carefully arranged, without a wedding ceremony, but also with domestic disputes! The young horses are treated equally irrespective of their sex, their grazing is controlled and exercise is encouraged. The competitive sports are rather Spartan in their characteristics.

COMMENT
- The Yahoo woman who makes the lustful attack on Gulliver is not a red-head but dark haired and a direct comparison with Jonathan Swift's admirer the Duchess of Somerset.
- Gulliver appears superior to the Yahoos, but inferior to the Houyhnhnms.

GLOSSARY   **jointures** dowries – money given to arrange a marriage
                       settlements financial arrangements

CHAPTER 9

The horses use the Yahoo for haulage, just as we use horses.

We are introduced to a council meeting which is involved in the same debate as to the origin and future of the Yahoos. The master, who remembers Gulliver's story of castrating horses, suggests that the young Yahoos should be gelded.

The Houyhnhnms have no need of books, their past is simply remembered, they have no need of medicine as their wounds need little attention. Poetry is limited, and their study of astronomy is limited to the sun and the moon. The Houyhnhnms build houses that are made of wattle and well constructed and carry their tools in their fetlocks. They are not frightened or apprehensive about dying; they visit their friends to say goodbye prior to their death. The only negative word in their language is 'Yahoo'.

COMMENT
- Jonathan Swift has a passion for writing, history and poetry. These are denounced in this chapter, as the perfect world of the Houyhnhnms does not study these topics.

GLOSSARY   **commerce** communication

CHAPTER 10

Gulliver has settled into a simple life. He has made chairs, clothes and found simple foods very enjoyable, especially honey. Gulliver is frequently in his master's company, where he learns to hate his own race. He now looks on his own kind as 'Yahoos in shape and disposition' (p. 327). He even goes as far as to adopt some horsey habits: he trots and neighs. However the Council of the Houyhnhnms has decided that Gulliver must leave and the grey horse has reluctantly agreed that Gulliver must leave also. There are fears that if he stays he will organise the Yahoos into some kind of mutiny. Gulliver is shocked by the news; interpreting it as nothing more than a death sentence. He tells the Houyhnhnms that if he does survive he will be destined to live a contemptible life.

What does Gulliver promise to do when he gets home?

The devoted sorrel nag and Gulliver build a canoe out of wattle and Yahoo skins; it has a sail and paddles. The Yahoos help Gulliver take it to the beach. A tearful farewell concludes this chapter. Gulliver is allowed to kiss his master's hoof.

COMMENT
- Note the very drastic contrasts in this chapter between the virtuous Houyhnhnms and the savage Yahoos.
- Note the extraordinary mark of distinction in Gulliver being allowed to kiss the horse's hoof, and the use of Yahoo skins as hide to cover the canoe. Aren't these the wrong way round?

ticking linen material
gibers jeerers
poxes diseases
pravity depravity

CHAPTER 11

As Gulliver leaves he hopes to find a deserted island where he can live without corruption. He is sailing in the direction of Western Australia; he finds a rocky inlet and beaches the canoe there. Naked savages occupy the island. After only three days a landing party

How effective is the Captain's attempt to rehabilitate Gulliver?

takes him aboard a Portuguese vessel. The sailors realise he is European by the colour of his skin but are confused by his strange dress and question him. The captain of the ship, Don Pedro de Mendez, is 'a very courteous and generous person' (p. 335). Gulliver perceives the crew as Yahoos and attempts to jump overboard. The captain takes him to Lisbon and then home to his wife and family. We are told the sight of his family fills him with 'hatred, disgust and contempt' (p. 338). Gulliver is unable to touch any of his family and ensures they do not use his supper plate. He buys two young horses and he spends four hours each day talking to them. Gulliver now prefers the company of his horses or his groom to that of his wife.

COMMENT

- The Portuguese captain is probably the nicest character in the book. He takes considerable time and patience to understand Gulliver.

CHAPTER 12

Jonathan Swift concludes his novel by testifying that Gulliver's travels are the truth and not a fiction to amuse. Gulliver says 'I rather chose to relate plain matter of fact in the simplest manner and style, because my principal design was to inform, and not to amuse thee' (p. 340). He goes on to say he has written without a view to making money, quite simply to inform the public. He quotes from Virgil's *Aeneid*, that 'fortune has made him wretched, but has not made him a liar'. This is **ironical** (see Literary Terms) as it follows a lie about the Trojan Horse: does this mean that Jonathan Swift with tongue-in-cheek is declaring loudly that Gulliver's story is indeed a work of fiction? In the account of the Houyhnhnms we are asked to question our own vices.

Gulliver feels the Brobdingnagians are the least corrupted of the Yahoos; he then goes on to discuss

CHAPTER 12 continued

the possible colonisation of these countries. Gulliver
contrasts the tyrannical European colonies with a
beneficial invasion of Houyhnhnms. He continues to
give the reader a résumé of Houyhnhnm features in
Yahoo surroundings.

COMMENT
- The reader wants to learn more of Gulliver and his
  family; instead we are only asked to believe in the
  author's honesty.
- The encounter with the Houyhnhnms has left
  Gulliver with a sympathy for horses.
- Jonathan Swift finishes the book by giving the reader
  insight into Gulliver. We are left with a picture of
  pride, vanity and misanthropy to such a huge degree
  that it becomes almost comic; the character is now
  unrealistic.

GLOSSARY   *Recalcitrat undique tutus* to find safety by kicking out in all
            directions
            docible teachable or biddable

A *'To whom' does the following refer.*

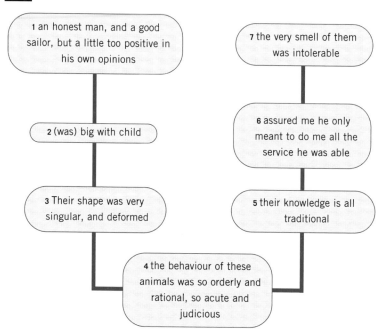

1 an honest man, and a good sailor, but a little too positive in his own opinions

7 the very smell of them was intolerable

2 (was) big with child

6 assured me he only meant to do me all the service he was able

3 Their shape was very singular, and deformed

5 their knowledge is all traditional

4 the behaviour of these animals was so orderly and rational, so acute and judicious

Check your answers on page 89.

 B *Consider these issues.*

a The descriptions given of the accommodation and diet of the Houyhnhnms and those of the Yahoos: what are Jonathan Swift's intentions?

b What comparison Jonathan Swift intended us to draw from the debate on the extermination of Yahoos.

c Why Jonathan Swift gives human intellect to the horses and animal-like instinctive behaviour to the Yahoos. What do you feel Jonathan Swift is trying to do?

d The appropriateness of this quotation: 'a traveller's chief aim should be to make men wiser and better, and to improve their minds' (p. 340).

e The ways in which Gulliver's experience with the Houyhnhnms changes him.

PART THREE

COMMENTARY

THEMES

POLITICAL REFERENCES

Some parallels may be drawn between *Gulliver's Travels* and the politicians and political events of the times. The table opposite may help us to better understand some of the characters, events and opinions represented by Jonathan Swift.

SATIRE AND IRONY

It is not what is said that is important but what is inferred.

Frequently at this time literature was used as a political tool. It was used to send messages, make people think, and to make subversive criticism of monarchy, political parties, or religious factions. To do this effectively the author used **satire** and **irony** (see Literary Terms). This is where writing exposes the follies of human behaviour by presenting it as absurd or ridiculous (satire) or saying one thing and meaning another (irony).

The whole of *Gulliver's Travels* is ironical. The Englishman in the strange land surrounded by miniature beings is no more than an outsider. In the first book we see ourselves as one of these miniature beings. In the second book Gulliver is overwhelmingly human, with human weakness, distorting the truth, and human strengths, the positive oration. In the last book the situational satire moves beyond our feeling comfortable with it. In this book there is a complete transposition of horse and man. We see a civilisation

Man and horses change places!

that is pure and rational. Fraud, deceit, illness, or greed have not influenced it.

Jonathan Swift writes of all social injustices and personal discomfort. Often the writing is with biting

George I	similar to the **Emperor** of Lilliput – both enjoyed music and military parades
Walpole	he was once helped by the Duchess of Kendal to return to power; could be **Flimnap**, the Treasurer, who was saved by one of the King's cushions
Walpole's wife	said to be unfaithful – could be likened to **the wife of the Prime Minister** of Laputa
Whigs	a political party referred to as **Slamecksan** in the novel
Tories	a political party referred to as **Tramecksan** in the novel
Catholics	referred to as **Big-Endians** in the novel
Protestants	referred to as **Little-Endians** in the novel
The Whig Committee of Secrecy 1715, which inquired into the Treaty of Utrecht	this could be compared with the **Articles of Impeachment** against Quinbus Flestrin
The Order of the Garter, the Bath and the Thistle, all orders of merit in Jonathan Swift's time	these are referred to as **'coloured threads'** in the novel
English oppression of Ireland	this could be reflected in **the oppressive behaviour of Laputa to Balnibarbi**
Absentee landlords in Ireland, actually living in England	could be compared to **Ministers' Estates in Balnibarbi**
The failure of the Irish agricultural system	referred to as **'soil badly cultivated'**
Halley's Comet, 1682 – a spectacular sight, said to be an omen	referred to as **'the last comet'**
The Royal Society – frequently ridiculed by cynics	like the **Academy of Projectors**

sarcasm but sometimes with violent explosions of anger, frequently with quiet ridicule. However he does this, the intention is the same and he urges the reader to really think about the effect of these views.

We are asked to consider lust, pride and conceit.

Jonathan Swift intends that even the most far-fetched of his characters is meant to remind the reader of human weaknesses; lust, barbarism, pride and conceit. Often Jonathan Swift gives us direct comparisons. Two good examples of these are the people in the Court at Lilliput and their antics to procure promotion, and the people in the Academy at Lagado and their time consuming and worthless research.

As we travel through each book the humanity becomes more degenerate and despicable and we are left to face ourselves in the Yahoo, whereas the well-bred horse portrays the superior, sensitive, intelligent and virtuous characteristics.

In the world of Lilliput we view with some amusement how meaningless the lives at court are. The ceremonies become silly, the awarding of honours meaningless, and the political differences completely comic when we consider such rivalry over which end an egg is eaten

Swift points to the futility of all wars.

from! The whole 'seriousness' of Lilliput is reduced to merely a side-show where we, the spectators, see the action for what it really is, nonsense.

An alternative environment, that of Brobdingnag, suggests a complete contrast. The tiny become giants and we see things from exactly the opposite perspective. The close-up pictures of skin, nipple and food, repulse the reader and we are left to question how we judge beauty and elegance. Other people become physically unattractive to Gulliver in Brobdingnag, just as he himself became socially and intellectually unattractive in Lilliput. In the former the characters are ridiculed, in the latter it is society as a whole which is held up to ridicule.

Ironically, now Gulliver is twelve times smaller, it is his people who are ridiculed by the King of Brobdingnag, just as he, Gulliver has ridiculed the antics of the Lilliputians.

Books I and II reverse the perspectives completely. Gulliver is a Brobdingnagian in Lilliput. Here among miniature men he witnesses their spite and envy. Contrary to this, Gulliver is a Lilliputian in Brobdingnag and witnesses, despite his fears, the generosity and benevolence of the giants. Indeed it is only in this book where Gulliver holds a tender relationship with Glumdalclitch, in an 'Alice in Wonderland' kind of way.

Consider how this focuses on the importance of physical size.

The use of the sizing up and down by a factor of twelve demonstrates the inconsequence of size and focuses us back to the fact that we are what we believe, not how we eat or live in physical terms. Only wisdom, integrity, honesty and loyalty are independent of size.

In Book III Jonathan Swift turns his attention to these virtues or lack of them. The focus of Laputa is intellectual and cognitive. In Book III we need to consider four main areas of satire. Jonathan Swift attacks the false learning and bizarre research by making the projectors eccentric and obsessive. He uses the oppression of Balnibarbi by Laputa to remind the reader of the Anglo-Irish issues. He refers to unrewarded efforts and political corruption and even the desire for eternal life by using the Struldbruggs. Throughout all of Book III the reader is forced to use his or her intellect.

In the fourth book, we are given a contrast awful in its extremities. The human Yahoo with its bestiality is compared to the horse-like Houyhnhnms who display virtues far above those observed in human society. The satire in this book is aimed at the Yahoos; Jonathan Swift uses them as a **device** (see Literary Terms) to explain how awful the human race really is. The comparisons are individual and in political groups. The comparisons are frequently odious, and in some cases indecent. Jonathan Swift uses all of the skills in his power to demonstrate the gross behaviour of the human being.

LANGUAGE & STYLE

Satire and **irony** (see Literary Terms) run throughout all four books (see also Themes where the satirical style of *Gulliver's Travels* is dealt with).

Jonathan Swift said 'Satire is a sort of glass wherein beholders do generally discover everybody's face but their own; which is the chief reason … that so very few are offended with it' (*Battle of Books*, 1696).

It is his gentle use of adventure in criticising his England, Ireland, and government which makes Jonathan Swift's novel work on two levels.

Gulliver's Travels is a first person narrative, that is Gulliver tells us the story, interprets for us judgements and helps us form opinions. The difficulty for the reader of a text like this is that other characters remain

This book is more than just a story – it makes a social comment.

ill-defined and in the background. The plot is the strongest feature, from life with miniature men to the land of giants, to the land of academics and finally to the intellectuals. We are given not only the exciting action but also Gulliver's reflections on what he hears and sees and also his views on life back home in England.

Nonsense words add credibility to the bizarre story.

The language seems strange to our ears, particularly the descriptions of life at sea which are portrayed in so much detail. However the story transcends three hundred years and the language does not inhibit our understanding of what is happening.

Another level of language is at work here and that is the level of nonsense words – i.e. Big-Endians, Little-Endians, Struldbruggs, Tramecksans, Slamecksans, Yahoos – a deliberate invention to increase the mystery and perhaps also to add a little humour. It is well to remember that at the time of the publication, readers actually believed the stories and frequently looked up these islands in their atlas.

Some critics feel that there may be a similarity with the *Odyssey* by Homer (*c.*850BC) or *Tom Jones* by Henry Fielding (1749). *Gulliver's Travels* may be likened to Christian's journey in *The Pilgrim's Progress* (1684) and Robinson Crusoe's adventures (1719), but none of these display the deep satire and irony of this unique text.

CHARACTERS

GULLIVER

Gulliver plays a more prominent part in Books I and II. He is treated ceremoniously and with high regard by the Lilliputians, and with affection by the Brobdingnagians who regard him almost as an interesting pet. The high regard held by the Lilliputians is not seen in Book III where the Laputans quite simply ignore him. The only interaction he has in Book III is with the academics of Lagado, and then only to demonstrate the magical understanding these people seem to have of life and logic. By Book IV Gulliver is looked upon suspiciously, almost with disgust as he is regarded as a kind of Yahoo.

Can Gulliver be considered as a symbol of honesty?

Gulliver may be compared with Christian in *The Pilgrim's Progress* (by John Bunyan, 1684) and Robinson Crusoe in *The Life and Adventures of Robinson Crusoe* (by Daniel Defoe, 1719). Each book was written by a Puritan at about the same time. The characters were used to portray various types of struggle: Christian's struggle over salvation; Crusoe's struggle over daily hardships and eventually for survival; and Gulliver's over the political and moral problems facing government. It could be said that each of these characters becomes responsible for his own actions and adventures, each represents true honesty, and each even wins the devotion of an equally honest friend in Hopeful, Man Friday and Glumdalclitch.

Gulliver is portrayed as an honest, educated man determined to earn a living as a ship's surgeon at sea. He is philosophical about the adventures and mishaps he encounters. He faces the new and wonderful people with genuine interest and relays details refreshingly and without malice. It is Gulliver's attention to detail which gives us, the reader, an insight into the wonderful worlds Gulliver visits. We see, hear and experience through Gulliver's senses. It is this which helps us to decide very effectively about Gulliver's personality, his likes and dislikes, his joys and fears, his morality and political preferences.

Gulliver has a sense of honour, he has left his family in order to provide for them. He is reminded of his oath to the Emperor and feels embarrassed when he is publicly displayed. His respect for royalty is witnessed with his dealings with the princess. Gulliver gently kisses her hand and bends low. This is linked with his sense of patriotism; for Gulliver, England is best. When he explains to the King about England he tends to ignore the weaknesses of the English system of law and government. We know Gulliver is interested by politics, frequently holding conversations on biased appointments, irrelevant wars and dishonest elections.

Note Gulliver's interest in politics. We also learn he has anti-militaristic views and is especially critical of people who fight simply for money. Yet despite this view we learn that Gulliver himself must have been trained to use hand sword, staff and pistols because he uses all these effectively on his journeys.

Gulliver is above all else a good conversationalist, always ready to ask and answer questions; he has an enquiring mind and is keen to learn. This is evidenced by his learning new languages, his ability to make accurate measurements and his interest in history. Gulliver takes easily to all spheres of society, whether it be Emperor or King, tradesman or servant. He is always ready to help or give helpful advice where he thinks it will be valued.

If we have a criticism of Gulliver it is that he does not seem to have deep affection for his wife and child. We are told in Book IV 'I left my poor wife big with child' (p. 267) and when he returns home she kisses him and Gulliver is appalled, 'having not been used to the touch of that odious animal for so many years' (p. 339).

Indeed, he clearly leaves the adventures for a warm relationship with the inhabitants of his stable. About his groom, Gulliver says, 'I feel my spirits revived by the smell he contracts in the stable' (p. 339).

Gulliver as an ironic device Gulliver is used as **narrator** (see Literary Terms); his view is innocent, unemotional, clearly focused and unambiguous (see **ambiguity** in Literary Terms). At the same time as the observations we are allowed an insight into Gulliver's (or Jonathan Swift's) opinions. Gulliver, educated and rational, inspires our confidence from the first. He supplies us with detailed observations that add to the **verisimilitude** (see Literary Terms) of the plot.

Generally he portrays the scene in a positive light, and wishes to be perceived in the same way; an example of this is when Gulliver displays his clemency by sparing the ruffians and is commended for his actions at court. Gulliver has impeccable and genteel manners, made laughable by the differences in size in both Lilliput and Brobdingnag.

Gulliver appears to be a gentleman.

Jonathan Swift uses Gulliver as an example of a 'good' human being, but throughout the book we are continually asked to question how good human beings really are. Gulliver horrifies the King with the secret of gunpowder yet is horrified that promotions in Lilliput rely on whether the applicant has gymnastic skills! In Book IV it is Yahoo skins Gulliver uses for his canoe not the horse skins in common use by his civilisation.

Jonathan Swift uses Gulliver to deny accusations or to embarrassingly embellish an argument only to give us an even clearer understanding of the human frailties being portrayed. So the 'innocent' Gulliver is used as a catalyst to allow the reader a deeper understanding of issues. An example of this is clothing, which is all that distinguishes Gulliver from the Yahoo.

Gulliver is used to deliver a technique of reversal or verbal **irony** (see Literary Terms). In Book I we are told of the Emperor's qualities, all of which are the opposite of George I's characteristics. In Book II Gulliver's praise of his country is overexaggerated, and therefore lacks credibility. Very often one seemingly credible paragraph is followed by another which makes us reconsider what we have already read. This is a particular **device** (see Literary Terms) in Book IV which engages the reader to reflect upon what they have read. An example of this is when Gulliver explains what horses are used in for in England and shocks the Houyhnhnms.

Note the shocking moments to make us think!

Gulliver is also used to shock and embarrass us. Gulliver urinates and moves his bowels all in graphic detail. Gulliver describes his being stripped naked and riding upon the nipple of a Maid of Honour. He describes the texture of skin and obscene eating habits in magnified detail and culminates in a graphic portrayal of the Yahoos. Jonathan Swift makes us stop to reflect upon the unspoken natural moments of our lives which link us more to animals than we care to admit. Indeed most readers identify, as Gulliver did, with the Houyhnhnms. This must be the absolute irony, as irony is impossible in the Houyhnhnms' society because 'the thing which is not' is not meant as a deception. In Book IV the **satirical** (see Literary Terms) ingredient is sarcasm and the grey 'master' frequently uses this. He describes the Yahoo as 'a sort of animal'.

Some examples of irony are easy to identify:
- 'I was demanded to swear to the performance of them; first in the manner of my own country, and afterwards in the method prescribed by their laws' (p. 78)
- 'These **unhappy** people were proposing schemes for persuading monarchs to choose favourites upon the score of their wisdom, capacity and virtue' (p. 232)
- 'The last of these (mathematics) is wholly applied to what may be useful in life, to the improvement of agriculture and all mechanical arts; so **that among us it would be little esteemed**' (p. 176).

There are also many examples of sarcasm – for example:
- 'And it would be **hard** indeed, if so **remote** a Prince's notions of virtue and vice were to be offered as a standard for all mankind' (p. 174).

GLUMDALCLITCH

Glumdalclitch is a child of nine who appears in Book II and acts as a carer for Gulliver. She acts as go-between for Gulliver in this land of Giants. She makes his clothes, teaches him some of the language, cares for his well-being and helps make him a bed. Glumdalclitch regards Gulliver as her own and cares for him as a child would a doll, with tenderness and constant interest. Glumdalclitch is allowed to care for Gulliver at all times and is therefore allowed into court with him and live with the Queen. We are led to believe that Glumdalclitch is honest, moral and dedicated. She does tell tales of Gulliver's behaviour just as any nine year old would, but it is without malice, indeed she worships Gulliver and is heartbroken at the final parting.

SETTINGS

LILLIPUT

The land of 'little' people

We are taken quickly to the country of Lilliput via a shipwreck, and are told of Gulliver's background succinctly; he is educated, a ship's doctor and much travelled.

Lilliput is an island to the northwest of Australia separated from Blefuscu by only a narrow strip of water, through which Gulliver is able to wade. The capital of Lilliput is Mildendo.

Lilliput has a severe system of laws and punishment. People who are traitors are put to death; as are people who wrongly accuse others. Victims of false accusation are compensated. The law-abiding are rewarded by being granted money or privileges at court. The statue of Justice holds a bag of gold and a *sheathed* sword, **symbolic** (see Literary Terms) of the way in which peace is valued.

Satire is introduced gradually in Lilliput sometimes at Gulliver's expense; often at the expense of the Lilliputians. Gulliver is tied by 'slender ligatures' (p. 55) and while he is being fed he considers himself 'bound by the laws of hospitality' (p. 59).

The Emperor is intended to represent King George I, who reigned at Jonathan Swift's time, and there are also many resemblances to King George in the description of the King of Laputa, whom we meet later.

Lilliput is portrayed as a miniature England of Jonathan Swift's day. The Emperor takes advice from his first minister as the King would have taken advice from the Whigs. Intermittent warfare with Blefuscu adds a sense of insecurity to the lives of the Lilliputians.

Lilliputian solider

The nation is divided into two political parties. The Tramecksan, or High-Heels, are the biggest party, but the Slamecksan, or Low-Heels, are actually in power. Ironically, we are told that the heir to the throne, the young prince, wears one of each shoe and hobbles between the two parties. We are then introduced to Big-Endians, who follow the old religion and eat their eggs from the big end, and Little-Endians, who have claimed freedom to interpret 'convenient end', and open their eggs at the little end. They fight with each other about which end is the correct one.

The social strata of Lilliput

Gulliver takes pains to introduce us to social rank. He explains a Nardac is higher than a Clumglum. They all wear different coloured threads to denote various honours that have been bestowed upon them. Some of these honours are gained in the most astonishing way. There are competitions in creeping under or leaping

over a stick, rather like our high jump or limbo dancing.
There are also competitions in rope-dancing – these
enable poor as well as rich, educated as well as ignorant,
to compete for honour. The Secretaries of State, we are
told, accept money for their services. We also are
amazed that Royal Proclamations claim leniency has
been offered towards culprits, yet immediately there
follow the most severe sentences! Gulliver portrays a
regime that wants to be **seen** to be just, rather than one
that **is** just.

The people of Lilliput are presented to us 'en masse' as
spectators the massive Gulliver. We learn little of them
except that they are buried head-downwards because
their expectation of life after death is to be resurrected
upside down. We learn that children are educated in
institutions which are suitable for their intended

How hard is it
being a child in
Lilliput?

careers, and that the children's handwriting slopes from
one corner to another. Designations are made at birth
for the type of education. The parents are expected
to make a contribution towards this education not
simply by paying the school fees, but by also
contributing towards their upkeep. In these institutions
the children are prevented from having regular contact
with their parents where they may be spoiled and
bad habits develop, and are praised for their positive
characteristics. The boys and girls who will go into
trade leave school earlier than the others into a kind of
apprenticeship. Girls receive a more limited education
than the boys, and are not encouraged to wear jewellery
or to listen to gossip.

The children of the labourers are not educated at all,
but go to work as soon as they are old enough. When
they are sick or very old they are specially cared for by
the State. Begging is not done in Lilliput. Jonathan
Swift gives us a contrast with Brobdingnag where
Gulliver sees beggars in the streets.

Everyone and everything is one twelfth of the 'normal' size in Lilliput. Jonathan Swift has taken great care to scale down effectively all that we are asked to witness. Note how the snuffbox Gulliver owns is seen as a silver chest and his gun a hollow iron pillar. Gulliver's ticking watch makes a loud noise in Lilliput. Jonathan Swift cleverly contrasts the difference in size. He portrays Gulliver carrying tiny people, striding across their houses and being unable to see some tiny details of Lilliputian life. An example of this is someone threading a needle.

BROBDINGNAG

Brobdingnag is a deliberate contrast to Lilliput. Here Gulliver finds himself one twelfth of the size of the inhabitants. Even the smallest animals are huge in Brobdingnag and terrifying for Gulliver. Gulliver has close encounters with dogs, cats, wasps, a monkey, a frog and a snail. He develops a sense of revulsion for all these enlarged encounters, and recalls faulty complexions, sores, a bloody execution, and even the act of someone eating. A suckling baby and a beggar repulse Gulliver, and he describes these events in graphic detail.

Note the contrast here with Lilliput.

The reader is led to believe that Brobdingnag is a 'continent' in the North Pacific, some 6,000 miles long with an impassable range of mountains bordering the country on one side, and a harbourless rocky coastline on the other.

As a contrast to Lilliput, there are no political parties. Instead, there is simply a three-tier society of King, nobles and commoners (the working-class people). These common people display honest human weaknesses – greed and envy – and honest virtues, such as common sense, shrewdness and an avoidance of gossiping and trouble making. Everything here is very simplistic. The army is a left over from earlier civil wars; the libraries are sparse and few in number. The only subjects taught are morality, history, poetry and practical mathematics. Some of the cleverer individuals serve at court and advise the King.

Brobdingnag boasts a narrow-minded but practical King who listens patiently to Gulliver's description of England and makes careful notes before he cross-examines and questions him. Gulliver tries to respond as fully and as positively as he can to this questioning but the King arrives at his own conclusion: 'I cannot but conclude the bulk of your natives to be the most pernicious race of little odious vermin' (p. 173).

This simple philosophy almost refreshing!

Despite this narrow-mindedness, the nation seems well governed and orderly. The King seems to concentrate on the physical realities rather than on political intrigue; he rules by the adage that he could 'make two ears of corn, or two blades of grass to grow upon a spot of ground where only one grew before' (p. 176). These simple people confound Gulliver in that they are unable to understand the notion of national debt or the variety of differences in religious or political opinions.

LAPUTA

Jonathan Swift used the third book as a 'bridge' between the two almost ideal but opposite worlds of Brobdingnag and the land of the Houyhnhnms. Laputa is an island civilisation that floats through the air somewhere described vaguely as above the mid-Pacific. It is, we are told, a circular plate or saucer shape, three hundred yards thick and four-and-a-half miles in diameter. The underside of the island is reflective and smooth. Water gathers in the concave shape above to make four lakes, which provide drinking water.

The whole island is steered by a magnet which is in the Astronomer's Cave and is six yards long. The motion is very smooth and, according to Gulliver, hardly noticeable. The magnet is caused by a set of controls either to be attracted or repulsed away from the earth's surface. The magnetic influence of the mineral below ground only works for up to four miles and does not work beyond the natural boundaries of the King's realm. This is useful in suppressing riots in neighbouring territories by parking above the territory and preventing the rain and sunshine reaching the ground below. The island people are also at liberty to bomb or even flatten those below them. This makes them a controlling power.

This is a comment by Swift on what seemed to be important at the time.

The people who inhabit this island are preoccupied with mathematics and music. Even the food they eat is carved into mathematical or instrumental shapes. Their preoccupation with the 'music of the spheres', often playing for three hours at a time, enables them to make very complex mathematical calculations. Frequently they get these calculations incorrect and this gives a bizarre appearance to everyday objects that are incorrectly designed. These mistakes include their houses, furniture and clothing.

Laputa seems to have two main classes of people: scholars and commoners. The scholars have one eye turned inwards (introspective), and this makes them hold their heads on one side. The other eye is turned upward (astronomy). These scholars walk awkwardly and are clumsy.

Because these people are so absent-minded, they need servants called 'flappers' whose job it is to smack their masters with a bladder to attract their attention. When they greet each other they are seldom relaxed, always anxious about the state of the Sun, fearing an eclipse or a comet. The women also seem tense and hate this very idle if comfortable life. The women are frequently visited by 'gallants' from the world below.

BALNIBARBI

Balnibarbi lies on the main surface; it is larger than Laputa. Its capital is called Lagado. There is a poor picture painted of this place, with derelict housing and starving people. The agriculture has failed due to a series of misinformed projects, which took the place of the agriculture schemes which were in place and which had been working well before the interference of Laputian scholars.

The leaders of these projects, called the 'projectors', have visited Laputa and are thought to understand the mathematical theories. They are very critical of people who stick to old-fashioned and traditional methods. The projectors are based in 'The Academy of Projectors' in Lagado. The Academy has the reputation of housing senseless projects; for example, the extraction of sunshine from cucumbers, the burning of ice to make gunpowder, building houses from the roof downwards, and using blind people to mix paint. Other schemes included using pigs instead of manure, cobwebs instead of silk and, even more bizarre, feeding coloured flies to the spiders to save on buying dye to colour the silks!

These ideas are intended for us to question the real 'value' of the product.

The whole theme is of contradictory elements; an attempt to condense air, sowing chaff instead of corn, growing wool-less sheep and making cushions of marble.

Inside the academy are various 'schools':
• **The school of language**: this peculiar school discards

all words except nouns and uses objects instead of words in the 'universal language'. The philosophy behind this is that it will save men's lives but they would need to travel to communicate effectively.

- **The school of politics**: Ministers are appointed to this school by assessing their qualifications. Parliaments are likened to diseased bodies, and require a medical cure by regularly diagnosing and treating the Members of Parliament. In this school surgical fusion of half-brains in the same skull reconciles two 'schools of opinion' and therefore brings a peaceful political reconciliation. Political posts are obtained by a raffle system. Instead of being an active politician, the election relies simply on good luck. Neighbours are invited to assess each other's vices; these vices are then taxed accordingly. Other equally peculiar features are included in this assessment such as whether or not women are good-looking and smartly dressed.

Is Swift saying politicans are all diseased?

- **The department of speculative learning**: here the academics debate continually over their fantastic and astonishing projects. Here we are introduced to the 'word-frame', which contains all the words in the language. These are tiny pieces of wood and are connected by wires onto handles. To change the order of the words, the handles are moved; if this turns up a logical sequence of words, the phrases are written down. All these phrases are saved and are to be put into a compendium of all the available knowledge; this produces a very mixed and jumbled language.

A wonderful way to learn!

- **The school of mathematics**: problems are solved and written down on small biscuits called 'wafers'. The 'ink' used is a fluid which can be absorbed by the brain. To eat these solutions means the natural absorption of mathematical knowledge takes place through the diet.

GLUBBDUBDRIB

This is the land of magic and sorcerers and is referred to as 'The Island of Sorcerers'. The Prince who has a palace here is waited upon by dead servants who are required to work for twenty-four hours every three months. These servants respond to questions, but only about their own life-times, and are unable to talk about any other event in history, which frustrates Gulliver.

LUGGNAGG

The capital of this country is Trildrogdrib. Here there is a strange custom where visitors to court are asked to lick the dust before the Royal footstool. Favourable guests face a recently swept floor, whereas it is poisoned for those who are condemned.

The people in this land are courteous, good at conversing, and prefer even numbers to odd ones.

Gulliver's attitude changes very quickly.

The Struldbruggs are born with a red spot over the left eye, which as they grow becomes green, blue and then black. These strange 'people' are said to be 'Immortals'. They seem to be normal until thirty years of age, but then undergo a type of depression and lose any kind of regard for other people. They are jealous of the young, and recount exploits of their own youth. These exploits are frequently misremembered. These people 'suffer' longevity and are only able to estimate their age by the name of the last King before they entered into the

They are sentenced to life!

Struldbrugg stage, which takes place at about eighty years of age. They long for death, especially when at the age of eighty they are separated from their spouses and are regarded as being officially 'dead'. By the age of ninety they have declined; they are no longer able to read or converse, and they are seen by everyone as unpopular. This glimpse of longevity, and the pathetic figures it produces, horrifies Gulliver.

Laputa seems to be a caricature of Japan (as it was perceived in the eighteenth century), its customs, learning and industry.

THE LAND OF THE HOUYHNHNMS

In this land we are introduced to two very different races; one is a savage version of human beings, and the other an infinitely superior breed of horses. The horses are the ruling species and attempt to communicate with Gulliver. The first horse Gulliver encounters is the grey horse who becomes his 'master'. From this horse Gulliver learns that the horses are called 'Houyhnhnms' (which incidentally sounds like a horse's whinny), and the savage humans who live wild in the bush are called 'Yahoos'.

Yahoo

Gulliver lives here for about three years in a mud and wattle house erected for him by the Yahoos. The Houyhnhnms attempt to draw comparisons between themselves and their own form and that of Gulliver and his resemblance to the Yahoos; whom he comes to resemble even more when his clothes are worn and he is given fur and skins to wear instead. Gulliver persistently ignores the Yahoos, as he sees communication with these savages as a threat to his own safety.

Gulliver learns that the Houyhnhnms have a cultural background: they enjoy poetry, astronomy and have knowledge of herbal medicines.

The land is not portrayed in detail. The reader is given only a sketchy idea of what the country looks like with the mention of farm buildings, rivers and fields; in this part of the book the focus is on intellectuality.

Gulliver has been the only person to wear clothes; these are thought to be a way of his concealing the fact that he is a Yahoo. The horses feel that Gulliver smells like a Yahoo and that his clothes conceal his real identity. The Houyhnhnms are benevolent, kindly and are aware of the principles of friendship and good behaviour. These values are taught to the young who experience a regime of strict discipline. Lies are unknown and Gulliver takes trouble to explain what a lie is to them: it is understood by them as 'the thing which is not'. It is a strange moral dilemma that this exceptionally truthful species is not religious, has no faith and seemingly no real interest in the dilemmas faced by each other.

Note the importance of truth.

PART FOUR

STUDY SKILLS

HOW TO USE QUOTATIONS

One of the secrets of success in writing essays is the way you use quotations. There are five basic principles:

- Put inverted commas at the beginning and end of the quotation
- Write the quotation exactly as it appears in the original
- Do not use a quotation that repeats what you have just written
- Use the quotation so that it fits into your sentence
- Keep the quotation as short as possible

Quotations should be used to develop the line of thought in your essays.

Your comment should not duplicate what is in your quotation. For example:

> When Gulliver awakes he tells us that 'The chains that held my left leg were about two yards long, and gave me not only the liberty of walking backwards and forwards in a semicircle but ...'

Far more effective is to write:

> Gulliver wakens and finds he is chained by his left leg and is able to walk 'backwards and forwards in a semicircle'.

However, the most sophisticated way of using the writer's words is to embed them into your sentence:

> Gulliver's 'liberty' was restricted as he was chained by his left leg.

When you use quotations in this way, you are demonstrating the ability to use text as evidence to support your ideas - not simply including words from the original to prove you have read it.

Everyone writes differently. Work through the suggestions given here and adapt the advice to suit your own style and interests. This will improve your essay-writing skills and allow your personal voice to emerge.

The following points indicate in ascending order the skills of essay writing:

- Picking out one or two facts about the story and adding the odd detail
- Writing about the text by retelling the story
- Retelling the story and adding a quotation here and there
- Organising an answer which explains what is happening in the text and giving quotations to support what you write

....

- Writing in such a way as to show that you have thought about the intentions of the writer of the text and that you understand the techniques used
- Writing at some length, giving your viewpoint on the text and commenting by picking out details to support your views
- Looking at the text as a work of art, demonstrating clear critical judgement and explaining to the reader of your essay how the enjoyment of the text is assisted by literary devices, linguistic effects and psychological insights; showing how the text relates to the time when it was written

The dotted line above represents the division between lower and higher level grades. Higher-level performance begins when you start to consider your response as a reader of the text. The highest level is reached when you offer an enthusiastic personal response and show how this piece of literature is a product of its time.

Coursework essay

Set aside an hour or so at the start of your work to plan what you have to do.

- List all the points you feel are needed to cover the task. Collect page references of information and quotations that will support what you have to say. A helpful tool is the highlighter pen: this saves painstaking copying and enables you to target precisely what you want to use.
- Focus on what you consider to be the main points of the essay. Try to sum up your argument in a single sentence, which could be the closing sentence of your essay. Depending on the essay title, it could be a statement about a character: Gulliver starts out as a naïve but educated man, but finishes disillusioned and mentally disturbed; an opinion about setting: the more extraordinary the setting the more realistic the characters and plot; or a judgement on a theme: *Gulliver's Travels* is simply a satirical comedy.
- Make a short essay plan. Use the first paragraph to introduce the argument you wish to make. In the following paragraphs develop this argument with details, examples and other possible points of view. Sum up your argument in the last paragraph. Check you have answered the question.
- Write the essay, remembering all the time the central point you are making.
- On completion, go back over what you have written to eliminate careless errors and improve expression. Read it aloud to yourself, or, if you are feeling more confident, to a relative or friend.

If you can, try to type your essay, using a word processor. This will allow you to correct and improve your writing without spoiling its appearance.

Examination essay

The essay written in an examination often carries more marks than the coursework essay even though it is written under considerable time pressure.

In the revision period build up notes on various aspects of the text you are using. Fortunately, in acquiring this set of York Notes on *Gulliver's Travels*, you have made a prudent beginning! York Notes are set out to give you vital information and help you to construct your personal overview of the text.

Make notes with appropriate quotations about the key issues of the set text. Go into the examination knowing your text and having a clear set of opinions about it.

In most English Literature examinations you can take in copies of your set books. This in an enormous advantage although it may lull you into a false sense of security. Beware! There is simply not enough time in an examination to read the book from scratch.

In the examination

- Read the question paper carefully and remind yourself what you have to do.
- Look at the questions on your set texts to select the one that most interests you and mentally work out the points you wish to stress.
- Remind yourself of the time available and how you are going to use it.
- Briefly map out a short plan in note form that will keep your writing on track and illustrate the key argument you want to make.
- Then set about writing it.
- When you have finished, check through to eliminate errors.

To summarise, these are the keys to success:

- **Know the text**
- **Have a clear understanding of and opinions on the storyline, characters, setting, themes and writer's concerns**
- **Select the right material**
- **Plan and write a clear response, continually bearing the question in mind**

A typical essay question on *Gulliver's Travels* is followed by a sample essay plan in note form. You will need to look back through the text to find quotations to support your points. Think about your own ideas – the sample answer is only a suggestion and you may wish to ignore it and produce your own. But it is always a good idea to plan out your thoughts first – it will save you time and help you to organise your ideas. Remember – try to answer the question!

'*Gulliver's Travels* is a simple story, simply told for young children.' Discuss.

The essay falls into two main parts: yes, it is, and no, not just for young children. This works on two levels, an exciting adventure and a deep satire.

A: Yes   Young children enjoy the lively adventures. Look for what would be pleasing for them:

Lilliput:
- The tiny people
- The 'interview at court'
- The way practicalities are dealt with, i.e. food and drink and a bed for Gulliver

Brobdingnag:
- The concern young readers would have for the tiny Gulliver's safety
- The encounters with dog, boy, cat and wasps

Laputa:
- The weird inhabitants and their obsessions with experiments

Balnibarbi:
- Sympathy for the people who live in the shadow of Laputa

Glubbdubdrib/Luggnagg:
- The horror of being waited upon by dead people and even worse people left for ever waiting for death.

All of these scenes are portrayed by Gulliver in a very graphic and colourful way.

B: No   This book is meant for an adult audience. It is a satire by Jonathan Swift on the life and times he experiences. The events in the four books reflect Jonathan Swift's view of humanity. The reader needs to understand the historical background in order to really gain the full appreciation of this text. Issues to be explored in this part of the essay are:

Politics:
• Whigs and Tories represented by Slamecksans and Tramecksans

Church:
• The problems of differences of opinion in Lilliput and Blefuscu

Anglo-Irish problems:
• Reflected in the journey from Laputa to Balnibarbi, the nation of absentee landlords and neglect

Scientific research and The Royal Society:
• These are reflected in Laputa

FURTHER QUESTIONS & SUGGESTED ASSIGNMENTS

Make a plan as shown above and attempt these questions.

1 *Gulliver's Travels* is about the decline of humanity into savagery. What evidence is there in the text to support this idea?

2 How successful is *Gulliver's Travels*? Are Books I and II more believable than Books III and IV? If so, why?

3 Using *Gulliver's Travels* identify what Jonathan Swift considered to be good government and the

ideas he identified as being those of poor
government.

4 Gulliver is tested in a variety of ways; what does this
tell the reader of his character?

5 It is said that Jonathan Swift found 'much that was
ugly, little that was beautiful'. Using *Gulliver's
Travels* find evidence for this statement.

6 Compare the exploration of human nature in
Gulliver's Travels with that portrayed by either:

   a *An Inspector calls* by J.B. Priestley (1945)
   b *Journey's End* by R.C. Sherriff (1929)
   c *Blood Brothers* by Willy Russell (1985)
   d *Animal Farm* by George Orwell (1945)
   e *To Kill a Mockingbird* by Harper Lee (1960)
   f *Lord of the Flies* by William Golding (1954)

7 Compare the exploration of authority and
hierarchical structures in *Gulliver's Travels* with
either:

   a *Journey's End* by R.C. Sherriff (1929)
   b *Talking in Whispers* by James Watson (1983)
   c *Of Mice and Men* by John Steinbeck (1937)
   d *Lord of the Flies* by William Golding (1954)

8 Compare the use of satire and irony in *Gulliver's
Travels* with either:

   a *An Inspector calls* by J.B. Priestley (1945)
   b *Animal Farm* by George Orwell (1945)

9 Compare the BBC video presentation of *Gulliver*
with the text. Do you feel Gulliver is portrayed
more favourably in one than the other?

10 Compare the way the fantasy of *Gulliver's Travels* is
treated with one of the following:

   a *Alice in Wonderland* by Lewis Carroll (1862)
   b *The Queen and I* by Sue Townsend (1992)
   c *The Borrowers* by Mary Norton (1966)

PART FIVE

CULTURAL CONNECTIONS

BROADER PERSPECTIVES

Video A useful device to place the novel in its social and historical context is to look at the Channel 4 video starring Ted Danson (ISBN 5 014138 066574, VHS VC 6659). This extracts the main events and encounters; it is however not strictly in the same order and the text and some small details are omitted. The events in the text which shock the reader such as Gulliver's urinating over the palace and being stripped naked and placed on the Maid of Honour's breast are omitted. Other shocking revelations are similarly 'glossed over'. The use of Yahoo skins for the canoe is also omitted.

Other features are included in the video which are not present in the text. The bizarre commitment of Gulliver to an asylum and his subsequent 'trial by the doctors and rescue by his wife are not part of the original text.

Books The following books are useful for a more detailed literary criticism:

Gulliver's Travels: A Critical Study by W.A. Eddy (Princeton University Press, 1923)

The Prose Works of Jonathan Swift edited by Herbert Davis (Blackwell Publishers, 1987)

Jonathan Swift, a Hypocrite Reversed. A Critical Biography by David Nokes (OUP, 1985)

TV For examples of **satire** (see Literary Terms), in order to help you understand the concept, watch programmes like *Blackadder* on the BBC in which the characters are doing and saying one thing but are actually portraying something else entirely.

Film

The film *The Madness of King George* is also worth viewing (starring Nigel Hawthorne and written by Alan Bennett, 1994). It was thought a similar kind of illness affected Jonathan Swift. This illness had periods of madness interspersed with periods of very stark reality. This will also help set the historical background for the novel.

ambiguity to have a double meaning

denote to signify or mark out

device any literary method or technique can be called a device

irony saying one thing whilst meaning another (see Theme on Satire and Irony)

narrator the story teller

parody an imitation designed to mock or ridicule

satire a literary work in which vices, follies, stupidities, abuses for example are held up to ridicule and contempt

symbol where one thing is used to act or stand for another

verisimilitude the believability of a sequence or story

TEST ANSWERS

TEST YOURSELF (Book I)

A
1 Gulliver *(Chapter 1)*
2 The Hurgo *(Chapter 1)*
3 The great gate of the temple *(Chapter 1)*
4 The Emperor *(Chapter 2)*
5 Filmnap *(Chapter 3)*
6 Reldresal *(Chapter 4)*
7 Mildendo *(Chapter 4)*
8 Tramecksan *(Chapter 4)*
9 Blefuscudians *(Chapter 5)*

TEST YOURSELF (Book II)

A
1 The Farmer *(Chapter 1)*
2 Glumdalclitch *(Chapter 2)*
3 The Farmer *(Chapter 3)*
4 The King of Brobdingnag *(Chapter 3)*
5 The Queen of Brobdingnag *(Chapter 5)*

TEST YOURSELF (Book III)

A
1 Captain William Robinson *(Chapter 1)*

2 The Dutchman *(Chapter 1)*
3 Laputa *(Chapter 1)*
4 Laputians *(Chapter 2)*
5 A Flapper *(Chapter 2)*
6 The Academy *(Chapter 5)*
7 Glubbdubdrib *(Chapter 7)*
8 Luggnaggians *(Chapter 10)*
9 Struldbruggs *(Chapter 10)*

TEST YOURSELF (Book IV)

A
1 Captain Pocock of Bristol *(Chapter 1)*
2 Gulliver's wife *(Chapter 1)*
3 The Yahoos *(Chapter 1)*
4 The Houyhnhnms *(Chapter 1)*
5 The Houyhnhnms *(Chapter 9)*
6 Don Pedro *(Chapter 11)*
7 Gulliver's wife and family *(Chapter 11)*

Notes

GCSE and equivalent levels (£3.50 each)

Maya Angelou
I Know Why the Caged Bird Sings

Jane Austen
Pride and Prejudice

Alan Ayckbourn
Absent Friends

Elizabeth Barrett Browning
Selected Poems

Robert Bolt
A Man for All Seasons

Harold Brighouse
Hobson's Choice

Charlotte Brontë
Jane Eyre

Emily Brontë
Wuthering Heights

Shelagh Delaney
A Taste of Honey

Charles Dickens
David Copperfield

Charles Dickens
Great Expectations

Charles Dickens
Hard Times

Charles Dickens
Oliver Twist

Roddy Doyle
Paddy Clarke Ha Ha Ha

George Eliot
Silas Marner

George Eliot
The Mill on the Floss

William Golding
Lord of the Flies

Oliver Goldsmith
She Stoops To Conquer

Willis Hall
The Long and the Short and the Tall

Thomas Hardy
Far from the Madding Crowd

Thomas Hardy
The Mayor of Casterbridge

Thomas Hardy
Tess of the d'Urbervilles

Thomas Hardy
The Withered Arm and other Wessex Tales

L.P. Hartley
The Go-Between

Seamus Heaney
Selected Poems

Susan Hill
I'm the King of the Castle

Barry Hines
A Kestrel for a Knave

Louise Lawrence
Children of the Dust

Harper Lee
To Kill a Mockingbird

Laurie Lee
Cider with Rosie

Arthur Miller
The Crucible

Arthur Miller
A View from the Bridge

Robert O'Brien
Z for Zachariah

Frank O'Connor
My Oedipus Complex and other stories

George Orwell
Animal Farm

J.B. Priestley
An Inspector Calls

Willy Russell
Educating Rita

Willy Russell
Our Day Out

J.D. Salinger
The Catcher in the Rye

William Shakespeare
Henry IV Part 1

William Shakespeare
Henry V

William Shakespeare
Julius Caesar

William Shakespeare
Macbeth

William Shakespeare
The Merchant of Venice

William Shakespeare
A Midsummer Night's Dream

William Shakespeare
Much Ado About Nothing

William Shakespeare
Romeo and Juliet

William Shakespeare
The Tempest

William Shakespeare
Twelfth Night

George Bernard Shaw
Pygmalion

Mary Shelley
Frankenstein

R.C. Sherriff
Journey's End

Rukshana Smith
Salt on the snow

John Steinbeck
Of Mice and Men

Robert Louis Stevenson
Dr Jekyll and Mr Hyde

Jonathan Swift
Gulliver's Travels

Robert Swindells
Daz 4 Zoe

Mildred D. Taylor
Roll of Thunder, Hear My Cry

Mark Twain
Huckleberry Finn

James Watson
Talking in Whispers

William Wordsworth
Selected Poems

A Choice of Poets

Mystery Stories of the Nineteenth Century including The Signalman

Nineteenth Century Short Stories

Poetry of the First World War

Six Women Poets

York Notes Advanced (£3.99 each)

Margaret Atwood
The Handmaid's Tale

Jane Austen
Mansfield Park

Jane Austen
Persuasion

Jane Austen
Pride and Prejudice

Alan Bennett
Talking Heads

William Blake
Songs of Innocence and of Experience

Charlotte Brontë
Jane Eyre

Emily Brontë
Wuthering Heights

Geoffrey Chaucer
The Franklin's Tale

Geoffrey Chaucer
General Prologue to the Canterbury Tales

Geoffrey Chaucer
The Wife of Bath's Prologue and Tale

Joseph Conrad
Heart of Darkness

Charles Dickens
Great Expectations

John Donne
Selected Poems

George Eliot
The Mill on the Floss

F. Scott Fitzgerald
The Great Gatsby

E.M. Forster
A Passage to India

Brian Friel
Translations

Thomas Hardy
The Mayor of Casterbridge

Thomas Hardy
Tess of the d'Urbervilles

Seamus Heaney
Selected Poems from Opened Ground

Nathaniel Hawthorne
The Scarlet Letter

James Joyce
Dubliners

John Keats
Selected Poems

Christopher Marlowe
Doctor Faustus

Arthur Miller
Death of a Salesman

Toni Morrison
Beloved

William Shakespeare
Antony and Cleopatra

William Shakespeare
As You Like It

William Shakespeare
Hamlet

William Shakespeare
King Lear

William Shakespeare
Measure for Measure

William Shakespeare
The Merchant of Venice

William Shakespeare
Much Ado About Nothing

William Shakespeare
Othello

William Shakespeare
Romeo and Juliet

William Shakespeare
The Tempest

William Shakespeare
The Winter's Tale

Mary Shelley
Frankenstein

Alice Walker
The Color Purple

Oscar Wilde
The Importance of Being Earnest

Tennessee Williams
A Streetcar Named Desire

John Webster
The Duchess of Malfi

W.B. Yeats
Selected Poems

Chinua Achebe
Things Fall Apart

Edward Albee
Who's Afraid of Virginia Woolf?

Margaret Atwood
Cat's Eye

Jane Austen
Emma

Jane Austen
Northanger Abbey

Jane Austen
Sense and Sensibility

Samuel Beckett
Waiting for Godot

Robert Browning
Selected Poems

Robert Burns
Selected Poems

Angela Carter
Nights at the Circus

Geoffrey Chaucer
The Merchant's Tale

Geoffrey Chaucer
The Miller's Tale

Geoffrey Chaucer
The Nun's Priest's Tale

Samuel Taylor Coleridge
Selected Poems

Daniel Defoe
Moll Flanders

Daniel Defoe
Robinson Crusoe

Charles Dickens
Bleak House

Charles Dickens
Hard Times

Emily Dickinson
Selected Poems

Carol Ann Duffy
Selected Poems

George Eliot
Middlemarch

T.S. Eliot
The Waste Land

T.S. Eliot
Selected Poems

Henry Fielding
Joseph Andrews

E.M. Forster
Howards End

John Fowles
The French Lieutenant's Woman

Robert Frost
Selected Poems

Elizabeth Gaskell
North and South

Stella Gibbons
Cold Comfort Farm

Graham Greene
Brighton Rock

Thomas Hardy
Jude the Obscure

Thomas Hardy
Selected Poems

Joseph Heller
Catch-22

Homer
The Iliad

Homer
The Odyssey

Gerard Manley Hopkins
Selected Poems

Aldous Huxley
Brave New World

Kazuo Ishiguro
The Remains of the Day

Ben Jonson
The Alchemist

Ben Jonson
Volpone

James Joyce
A Portrait of the Artist as a Young Man

Philip Larkin
Selected Poems

D.H. Lawrence
The Rainbow

D.H. Lawrence
Selected Stories

D.H. Lawrence
Sons and Lovers

D.H. Lawrence
Women in Love

John Milton
Paradise Lost Bks I & II

John Milton
Paradise Lost Bks IV & IX

Thomas More
Utopia

Sean O'Casey
Juno and the Paycock

George Orwell
Nineteen Eighty-four

John Osborne
Look Back in Anger

Wilfred Owen
Selected Poems

Sylvia Plath
Selected Poems

Alexander Pope
Rape of the Lock and other poems

Ruth Prawer Jhabvala
Heat and Dust

Jean Rhys
Wide Sargasso Sea

William Shakespeare
As You Like It

William Shakespeare
Coriolanus

William Shakespeare
Henry IV Pt 1

William Shakespeare
Henry V

William Shakespeare
Julius Caesar

William Shakespeare
Macbeth

William Shakespeare
Measure for Measure

William Shakespeare
A Midsummer Night's Dream

William Shakespeare
Richard II

William Shakespeare
Richard III

William Shakespeare
Sonnets

William Shakespeare
The Taming of the Shrew

William Shakespeare
Twelfth Night

William Shakespeare
The Winter's Tale

George Bernard Shaw
Arms and the Man

George Bernard Shaw
Saint Joan

Muriel Spark
The Prime of Miss Jean Brodie

John Steinbeck
The Grapes of Wrath

John Steinbeck
The Pearl

Tom Stoppard
Arcadia

Tom Stoppard
*Rosencrantz and Guildenstern
are Dead*

Jonathan Swift
*Gulliver's Travels and The
Modest Proposal*

Alfred, Lord Tennyson
Selected Poems

W.M. Thackeray
Vanity Fair

Virgil
The Aeneid

Edith Wharton
The Age of Innocence

Tennessee Williams
Cat on a Hot Tin Roof

Tennessee Williams
The Glass Menagerie

Virginia Woolf
Mrs Dalloway

Virginia Woolf
To the Lighthouse

William Wordsworth
Selected Poems

Metaphysical Poets

York Notes – the Ultimate Literature Guides

York Notes are recognised as the best literature study guides.
If you have enjoyed using this book and have found it useful, you
can now order others directly from us – simply follow the ordering
instructions below.

HOW TO ORDER

Decide which title(s) you require and then order in one of the following
ways:

Booksellers
All titles available from good bookstores.

By post
List the title(s) you require in the space provided overleaf,
select your method of payment, complete your name and
address details and return your completed order form and
payment to:

> *Addison Wesley Longman Ltd*
> *PO BOX 88*
> *Harlow*
> *Essex CM19 5SR*

By phone
Call our Customer Information Centre on 01279 623923 to
place your order, quoting mail number: HEYN1.

By fax
Complete the order form overleaf, ensuring you fill in your
name and address details and method of payment, and fax it
to us on 01279 414130.

By e-mail
E-mail your order to us on awlhe.orders@awl.co.uk listing
title(s) and quantity required and providing full name and
address details as requested overleaf. Please quote mail
number: HEYN1. Please do not send credit card details by
e-mail.

York Notes Order Form

Titles required:

Quantity	Title/ISBN	Price

Sub total _____

Please add £2.50 postage & packing _____

(*P & P is free for orders over £50*) _____

Total _____

Mail no: HEYN1

Your Name _____

Your Address _____

_____

Postcode _____ Telephone _____

Method of payment

☐ I enclose a cheque or a P/O for £_____ made payable to Addison Wesley Longman Ltd

☐ Please charge my Visa/Access/AMEX/Diners Club card
Number _____ Expiry Date _____
Signature _____ Date _____

(please ensure that the address given above is the same as for your credit card)

Prices and other details are correct at time of going to press but may change without notice. All orders are subject to status.

☐ *Please tick this box if you would like a complete listing of Longman Study Guides (suitable for GCSE and A-level students)*

York Press

Longman

Addison Wesley Longman